Studies and documents on cultural policies

Recent titles in this series:

For a complete list of titles see page 88

# Cultural policy
## in Jordan

Hani Al-Amad

unesco

Published in 1981 by the United Nations Educational,
Scientific and Cultural Organization,
7 place de Fontenoy, 75700 Paris
Printed by Imprimerie des Presses Universitaires
de France, Vendôme

ISBN 92-3-101749-7
Arabic edition: 92-3-601749-5

# Preface

The purpose of this series is to show how cultural policies are planned and implemented in various Member States.

As cultures differ, so does the approach to them. It is for each Member State to determine its cultural policy and methods according to its own conception of culture, its socio-economic system, political ideology and technical development. However, the methods of cultural policy (like those of general development policy) have certain common problems; these are largely institutional, administrative and financial in nature, and the need has increasingly been stressed for exchanging experiences and information about them. This series, each issue of which follows as far as possible a similar pattern so as to make comparison easier, is mainly concerned with these technical aspects of cultural policy.

In general, the studies deal with the principles and methods of cultural policy, the evaluation of cultural needs, administrative structures and management, planning and financing, the organization of resources, legislation, budgeting, public and private institutions, cultural content in education, cultural autonomy and decentralization, the training of personnel, institutional infrastructures for meeting specific cultural needs, the safeguarding of the cultural heritage, institutions for the dissemination of the arts, international cultural co-operation and other related subjects.

The studies, which cover countries belonging to differing social and economic systems, geographical areas and levels of development, present, therefore, a wide variety of approaches and methods in cultural policy. Taken as a whole, they can provide guidelines to countries which have yet to establish cultural policies, while all countries, especially those seeking new formulations of such policies, can profit by the experience already gained.

This study was prepared for Unesco by Dr Hani Al-Amad of the University of Jordan.

The author is responsible for the choice and the presentation of the facts contained in this book and for the opinions expressed therein, which are not necessarily those of Unesco and do not commit the Organization.

# Contents

# Foreword

The history of Jordan as an independent state begins after the end of the First World War. Until 1918, the area east of the River Jordan was a part of geographical Syria, which formed part of the Ottoman State. The Arab princes of that state began to work for their independence, and the great Arab revolt, which began on 9 Sha'aban AH 1334 (10 June 1916) under the banner of the Sharif Husain bin Ali in Mecca, derived its impetus from the two fundamental principles of liberation and unification.

The defeat of the Ottoman State resulted in the formation of an Arab government under the Emir Faisal bin Husain in Damascus, whose administrative control extended over the area east of the Jordan. Less than two years later, the Allies put an end to this regime. Immediately after this, in March 1921, a state was formed in the area east of the Jordan under the Emir Abdullah bin Husain. He succeeded, after overcoming great difficulties and obstacles, in considerably advancing the reputation and strength of Jordan. He established a strong kingdom, which has progressed towards prosperity and assumed its rightful position in the community of nations.

Despite the fact that Jordan has been an independent and distinct political entity for less than sixty years, the country has roots which go far back to prehistoric times. Although there has been a long succession of political and military developments in Jordan, bringing with them rulers who had their centres of power both near by and far away, and though Jordan lies on a crossroads, the country has had a continuity of population which, inevitably, had a dominant influence in providing an unbroken line of cultural development.

With all this, Jordan did not witness any fundamental change in either its economic system or the cultural results thereof until after the great Arab revival which was sparked off by Husain bin Ali's revolt against the Ottoman State. Even until shortly before these events, the great majority, around 65 per cent, of the inhabitants of Jordan were farmers. Desert Bedouin made up 30 per cent and 5 per cent were craftsmen who lived in country villages or small encampments. Consequently, there were no significant means of education that could support the cultural movement; such elementary education as there was, was imparted in twenty-one schools staffed by twenty-nine teachers (male and female). The period of schooling at that time was six years, and instruction was given in the Turkish language. This was the position for ordinary education. The informal education imparted by the 'Koranic elementary schools' was still more rudimentary, pupils being given their certificate as soon as they were able to read, count and write simple words, and had read or learned by heart parts of the Holy Koran. When the Jordanian state was established, only a handful of individuals had had the benefit of an education even slightly higher than that mentioned above. The state was aware of the need to start a complete educational revival with the aim of providing, within the first fifteen years, a nucleus of clerical workers for the government system.

Educational conditions improved only after the promulgation of a Statute on Education (No. 2 of 1939) when an educational administration was set up in Jordan. This administration had the task of establishing, administering and generally supervising state schools; of encouraging scientific and literary movements, a scout movement and sports in schools; of promoting the fine arts and supervising general culture and public morals.

From its creation, the Jordanian state tried to ensure that, in its development, there was a balance between the actual condition of society and its spiritual heritage. The state therefore encouraged the historical continuity of the present, regarding the present as the natural product of the past. It also began to issue executive, administrative and financial precepts in order to consolidate its inherited cultural activity, to confirm its continuity and to guarantee its development. These precepts also aimed at encouraging the interaction of the various sectors of knowledge with each other on both the intellectual and the scientific levels, so that each sector could be of benefit, and so that scientific progress could be a source of every person's spiritual wealth.

It can be said that the unity of the two banks of the Jordan, which was constitutionally effected on 24 April 1950, was the starting-point for a comprehensive development such as the Kingdom had not known until the two banks were united in a single state on the basis of a constitutional, representative government, and of equality in respect of rights and duties. In fact, since 1948, the people of both banks had faced the danger of illegal Israeli occupation, together with the need which this challenge imposed for constant alertness in the military sphere.

But it was not military matters alone that claimed attention. The state was also deeply concerned with education, and gave high priority to social affairs, tourism and information. It is sufficient to mention that at the start of the 1950s, there was one radio set for every fourteen families, and the number of readers of the daily press in 1951 was not more than 5,000.

The contact and merging together of the two peoples had an effect on the social condition of Jordan. While the proportion of those engaged in agriculture fell to 45 per cent and the Bedouins to 26 per cent, the percentage of craftsmen and town-dwellers rose to 29. From the beginning of the 1950s, large numbers of the population were taken into military service. By the start of the 1960s, the city of Amman had undergone considerable development, enabling it to absorb more than a quarter of the population of Jordan. The result of the progress and prosperity which the country had witnessed in all spheres was reflected in every sector of the population, but some sectors, especially those in the major towns, enjoyed a greater share than others. This led to the establishment of new centres of permanent population, concentrated in new towns. It also led to population movements as people began to migrate from less developed to more highly developed areas.

These successive developments were also reflected in economic and cultural conditions. However, when Jordanian society was beginning to acquire a natural form as a result of the stabilization of economic, social and cultural conditions, these conditions were once more upset as a consequence of the Israeli occupation of 1967. This impelled more displaced Palestinians to leave their homes and take refuge on the East bank. Even so, the number of those displaced was not nearly so great as it had been in 1948, and Jordan did not undergo a fundamental change such as that which resulted from the first migration.

Once again, the seriousness of the situation which followed this second occupation confirmed the attitude which underlies the cultural concerns of the state. These concerns, in their widest sense, were bound up with the need to strengthen the nation's links with the land, and to ensure its defence. This is the attitude we find not only in school curricula but also in much of the cultural output of the kingdom and the occupied territories.

In fact, awareness of the situation engendered by the Israeli occupation in the region is not a new phenomenon. From the 1920s when the direction of certain events became clear, Jordanian literature began to take on a new dimension and to warn of the seriousness of these trends. As a result, writers and thinkers gave increasing attention to categories of cultural activity which concentrated on this subject; these categories included historical studies and poetic and narrative works mainly concerned with this idea. These preoccupations can be traced in the material which appeared in Palestine and Jordan before 1948, and in the material published after that date which concentrated on the Palestine problem.

One consequence of this was that the state took on the sponsorship of literature and art and the first cultural activity to result from the direct interaction of the land and the people. It is true that this interaction did not take place in isolation from foreign trends which affected the Arab world, nor from the Arab and Islamic cultural heritage and the economic conditions imposed by political circumstances and other social and military factors. State cultural sponsorship was carried out on a large scale. However, it did not aim at, or call for, the imposition of any particular course of action, being concerned rather with encouraging creative activity, irrespective of whether it was scientific, literary or artistic.

His Majesty King Hussein of the Hashemite Kingdom of Jordan has given special attention to the various aspects of culture. His Majesty's royal decrees have stipulated the need for unremitting attention to Arab and Islamic civilization; the dissemination of its heritage and attention to its ethical values; as well as faith in God and the Divine Ideals, pride in Arab values and spiritual ideals in all fields of conduct; fruitful co-operation with others, and adherence to the democratic system in human relations. For this purpose, His Majesty has given orders for compulsory education, the opening of centres of higher education, the expansion of university education and the dissemination of culture so as to make it the right of every citizen. The King has been the patron of organizations concerned with cultural affairs: the Ministry of Culture and Youth, the Ministry of Education and Instruction, the University of Jordan, the Ministry of Information, the University of Yarmouk, the Ministry of Tourism and Antiquities, the Ministry of Islamic Endowments and Religious Affairs, and centres concerned with culture for children, etc. He has given constant care and attention to all these organizations.

His Majesty translated his close concern for culture into action when he ordered the creation of a ministry specializing in this field. The Ministry of Culture and Youth was created in order to spread knowledge and culture among Jordanians, and to familiarize them with Arab and Islamic civilization and its message; to stimulate and disseminate the Arab heritage in the sciences, literature and the arts; to encourage talent; to sponsor writers and artists, and to support composition and publishing.

Thus, Jordan has made great efforts to provide cultural life with an organized framework. The system of organization was described in a statement made by the Minister for Culture and Youth in the National Consultative Assembly. In this statement, he indicated that the work of the ministry had the following aims: the invigoration of the Arab and Islamic heritage, which contributes to the creation of the Jordanian identity and the Arab community; the encouragement of an intellectual movement which assists the interaction between our own progress, the progress of the Arab community and the world as a whole; the encouragement of a movement in the graphic arts, sculpture, drama and music which benefits taste, raises the spirit, and contributes to building a high level of civilization in Jordan; the support of artists and intellectual trends among individuals and organizations; the encouragement of general aesthetic awareness in all its forms.

These aims, which the Ministry of Culture and Youth was set up to achieve, and which are considered as a charter for Jordanian cultural policy, harmonize completely with the plans of the state with regard to scientific culture, whether theoretical or applied. There is a group of statutes and laws which the state is energetically engaged in implementing, while keeping firmly in mind the freedom of art and literature, science and education. One of the important principles, which the state is trying to put into practice, is the consolidation of links between world culture and local culture, and between culture in the strict sense, on the one hand, and purely scientific culture, on the other.

We must note here some elements connected with cultural development, which have had a real effect on most areas of culture, and which were introduced in order to meet the needs of the developing society in respect of both scientific and human studies. Concern with the humanities led to the emergence of the University of Jordan and then of the University of Yarmouk. These two universities participated in the publication of studies connected with general matters. The relevance of these studies was such that one of them received the state prize granted by the Ministry of Culture and Youth for recognition of achievement in historical studies in 1978. The Royal Scientific Society was established in response to Jordan's need to adopt modern scientific techniques in order to solve its pressing problems in many areas. The society has published many scientific studies to assist the country's development in this field.

In preparing this monograph, a historical approach has been adopted. In tracing the course of various cultural manifestations, I have relied on the relevant statutes, laws and directives, as well as on the sources which can be found in the bibliography at the back of this book. I have divided the book into three principal sections. In the first, I have dealt with cultural evolution in the light of development plans. The second section discusses the various organizations concerned with cultural affairs, and the third section deals with the different aspects of cultural activity.

In this connection, I must offer my warmest thanks and gratitude to His Excellency the Minister for Culture and Youth, Sharif Fawwaz Sharaf, who entrusted me with the task of preparing this study when I was Director of the Department of Culture and Arts, and provided me with the necessary documentation, thereby greatly facilitating my task.

I must also thank the Director-General of the Department of Antiquities, the committee which drew up the report on the Ministry of Education and Instruction, the Director for Public Relations in the University of Jordan and the Director of the Princess Hayya Cultural Committee, who were kind enough to provide me with reports on their respective areas of responsibility.

I must also pay tribute to Professor Salim al-Khouri, Secretary-General of the National Committee for Education, Culture and Science in the Ministry of Education and Instruction, who provided me with valuable information which I trust has been turned to good account in this work.

# Cultural evolution in the light of development plans

During the period 1948–78, there were fundamental and comprehensive economic, social and cultural developments in Jordan. These developments can be divided into five distinct phases: 1948–61, 1962–66, 1967–72, 1973–75 1976–80. The first and second phases were characterized by high rates of development. The third phase which followed the June war of 1967, was characterized by a fall in the levels of economic development, while there was an advance in the levels of social and cultural development.

## The period 1948–61

Despite the difficult economic and population problems faced by Jordan after the 1948 catastrophe, the domestic product grew at a high rate, averaging 11.5 per cent per annum. This development took place in the context of relative stability of prices, which rose by about 2 per cent per annum. Thus there was a real increase in average individual income, at a rate of 6.6 per cent per annum. The public sector concentrated its development effort on providing and developing the essential economic infrastructure. It also expanded and developed educational and social facilities. This effort was reflected in the increase in the number of school enrolments which rose from 218,000 students for the 1954/55 academic year to 297,000 students in the 1961/62 academic year; i.e. an average rate of increase of 4.5 per cent per annum.

New schools were started, and a number of cultural associations were inaugurated, through the efforts of the public and private sectors. Books and periodicals were published by the private and public sectors, including the magazine *New Horizon*, which played an important part in general cultural life, and the magazine *Voice of a Generation*, published by the Irbid Secondary School. The Jordanian Broadcasting Organization was also able to create channels for communication with the Jordanian public

14

in the fields of culture, religion, education and entertainment. The creative arts were encouraged. Technical, industrial and agricultural exhibitions were held. Jordanian folk-singing and other activities were encouraged.

## The period 1962–66

This period saw an increasingly rapid pace of development in economic, social and cultural activity. While in the previous period, efforts had been concentrated on establishing the essential economic, social and cultural infrastructures, the approach adopted in this second period was designed to promote comprehensive development. This trend found expression in the preparation during 1962 of the 1963/67 Five-year Programme for Economic and Social Development (subsequently amended to become the 1964–70 Seven-year Programme for Economic Development). This phase was characterized by concentration on the development of productive capacity by completing the various projects which had been started. The total national income increased at a rate of 9 per cent per annum. The public and private sectors continued to expand educational and cultural services, and the number of pupils enrolled in the schools increased from 297,000 in the 1961/62 academic year to 440,000 in the 1966/67 academic year, i.e. at an average yearly rate of 8.2 per cent, compared with an average rate of population increase of 3 per cent. During this phase, the University of Jordan was inaugurated and took in a large number of students. The Department of Culture and Arts was also established and linked with the Ministry of Information. There was an increase in the rate of internal migration from the countryside to the towns, especially Amman, and Zarqa, twenty kilometres away. The Jordan Library Association was founded at this time. Directives were issued for the protection of sites, pastures and places of scenic beauty. Libraries were started for the private and public sectors. Numerous exhibitions of the creative arts were held. There was notable activity in the Jordanian theatre, which began to make progress and to show local, Arab and international plays.

## The period 1967–72

The June war of 1967 led to the occupation of the West bank of the kingdom. Following this, the rise in economic development stopped. Military mobilization increased at the expense of the development effort. A large number of development projects that had been decided on in the seven-year programme were cancelled. This led in particular to a considerable decline in the average rates of economic development. The rate of growth of the service sector fell to about 1 per cent per annum. The number of students in schools on the East bank increased from 287,000 in the 1967/68 academic year to 460,000 in the 1972/73 academic year, i.e. an average yearly rate of increase of 9.9 per cent. The inflow of displaced people from the occupied West bank and the Gaza strip was a contributory cause of this high rate of increase.

During this period, important cultural activities were undertaken by the University of Jordan. More faculties were established and many more students who had completed the secondary cycle were enrolled. The number of books written increased fivefold, and more than two-thirds of these books were disseminated in Jordan in the occupied West bank—an indication of the growing role of the press and of the increasing number of writers and readers. The Royal Scientific Society was established in 1970, and museums were founded. Archaeological excavations continued, the results being published in the *Annual of the Department of Antiquities*. There was increased awareness of archaeology in the fields of protection, maintenance, repair and improvement of historic monuments. Specialist works were published dealing with the national heritage. Traditional crafts were encouraged. The Jordanian theatre developed through the work of academic producers who produced their plays in the theatre of the Department of Culture and Arts and in the University Theatre. Jordanian television was able to play a decisive role in the fields of information, culture and entertainment. These were only some of the activities undertaken during this period.

## The period 1973–75

This period saw a resumption of the activities which had been interrupted by the June war and by subsequent events. Development plans during this period aimed to create 70,000 new jobs, to achieve an annual average growth in total production of 8 per cent, and to develop the various forms of economic, social and cultural activity. The demographic pattern during this time was characterized by an increase in the annual growth rate to 3.5 per cent and by an increasing tendency to concentration in three principal cities; Amman, Zarqa and Irbid, which absorbed about 62 per cent of the population. This increase produced strong pressure for the expansion of educational and social services. The Arab world as a whole saw a great expansion of development from 1973 onwards, accompanied by a rapid increase in the demand for educated personnel. Jordan was affected by this, and had to face the drain of its technical and professional expertise. This had the consequence of putting pressure on the Jordanian labour market and limiting the capacity for implementing and administering development projects.

However, this three-year plan did, in fact, achieve its objectives. There came to be complete confidence in the Jordanian economy, as well as a total conviction of the need for a social transformation to enable the country to become more capable of adapting to change and development, always remembering that the Jordanian citizen himself was the goal of development and the focus of all the efforts made by the state.

This confidence was reflected in cultural objectives, through the participation of the general public in cultural life. At this time, the benefits of the national culture began to be more widely shared, and a youth welfare organization was set up in addition to the youth centres which became available to Jordanian young people between the ages of 13 and 19 in all parts of the kingdom. At the start of 1974, a magazine called *Popular Arts* commenced publication, and the League of Jordanian Writers was formed in the same year. The theatre developed, and cultural agreements were signed between Jordan and the Arab nations, and other countries of the world. Those responsible for the popular heritage in the Department of Culture and Arts worked unceasingly to record new folklore material. Clubs were formed to preserve the popular heritage. The authorities paid increasing attention to archaeology. New libraries were started, and exhibitions were held of painting, sculpture, architecture, planning and industrial design. There was clear evidence of interest in traditional design and traditional industries. An association of traders in oriental works of art was formed. Popular melodies were developed, and Jordanian radio and television devoted special attention to children's music and songs, and other cultural and entertainment programmes for children. There were improvements in the performing arts for schoolchildren, together with attempts to establish a cinema club. The television and radio services showed interest in film libraries. The Jordanian press developed by improving its methods of production, increasing its range and doing everything possible to satisfy its readers.

### The 1976–80 Five-year Development Plan

The objectives of this plan reflect the need to achieve a fundamental change in economic, social and cultural structures. In the economic field, the plan aimed at an all-round increase in production and at the achievement of higher levels and more equitable distribution of the national income. It also aimed at a truly endogenous development, achieved independently of foreign assistance. This will be brought about by convincing each citizen that comprehensive development will create a complete nation.

The development strategy is founded on the need to develop social activity on the basis of a new concept which aims at the reorganization of society and the extension of effective participation of all sectors of the population, especially the work force; to increase the part played by women in bringing about comprehensive change and to help women in organizing and raising the general social level of the family. Scientific research must be used to deal with the problems faced by Jordanian society and the results of this study must be the basis of government policy in developing the

17

kingdom. The work of the various scientific research organizations must be co-ordinated.

The plan linked the demands of economic and social development with the planning of education and training of various kinds and levels, so that quantitative expansion would not be brought about at the expense of qualitative improvement. The plan also stressed the need to develop the content of education, to remove out-dated material from the curriculum and to emphasize the value and importance of manual work. It further called for the participation of both the teaching and the student body in the implementation of projects and for the linking of policy on university education and applied scientific research with the fundamental requirements of development. It likewise emphasized the importance of vocational training for women.

In the information field, the plan stressed the importance of guiding the citizen and animating his sense of citizenship; informing the public, through all the available media about development in every sphere; encouraging the production of domestic television programmes and marketing those programmes in other Arab countries; implanting in the citizen new and up-to-date social, economic, and cultural values; creating a centre for information and communication training, together with a documentation centre; establishing a department of programmes and news, and setting up four studios; and implementing a project for the televising of cultural programmes.

In the field of education, the plan indicated the necessity of expanding both vocational education at the secondary level and comprehensive secondary education; increasing the number of teachers and their level of qualification; undertaking research and studies with the aim of developing school curricula and textbooks; implementing projects for polytechnic centres, technical colleges, a hotel school, rural development centres and comprehensive secondary schools; expanding vocational training for boys and girls, and establishing more schools of industry, commerce and agriculture; and devoting particular attention to adult education and the elimination of illiteracy.

The plan called for the University of Jordan to improve the quality of higher education by increasing the use of modern applied techniques of instruction. The university was also requested to increase its student intake by opening new faculties such as the Faculty of Engineering, the Faculty of Law, the Faculty of Fine Arts and the Faculty of Sports. The plan asked the University to concentrate on technical education and to expand scientific research and study.

In the field of youth welfare, the plan aimed at creating conditions in which it would be possible to lay the foundations of sound social development; to confront numerous negative attitudes and superficial concepts; to strengthen the spiritual development of young people and to imbue them with feelings of pride in the nation and its culture, identity, heritage and

18

values; to provide the appropriate cultural climate for Jordanian youth and to widen the basis and scope of cultural activities; and to establish a sound and authentic cultural infrastructure. The plan called for the establishment of a youth welfare organization to be responsible for establishing additional youth centres in towns and villages; carrying out programmes and establishing study groups in conjunction with the Ministry of Education and Instruction and the Ministry of Culture; constructing sports grounds and developing public cultural facilities generally; and helping to promote the inculcation of basic cultural skills such as reading and writing, and the development of different hobbies. The organization will also aim at implementing the plans for a Faculty of Sports in co-operation with the University of Jordan and the youth associations in the major cities, and at providing vocational training for young people.

In the field of tourism and archaeology, the plan aimed to stimulate tourism by creating incentives to attract tourists and by encouraging internal tourism so as to increase revenue from this source; to develop tourist facilities in the kingdom and to preserve the historical, cultural and aesthetic environment by implementing plans for national parks. The objectives which are laid down for the Department of Antiquities confirm the need for protecting, maintaining and repairing archaeological monuments; developing the necessary technical facilities for this purpose; disseminating awareness of archaeology and publicizing the importance of the archaeological heritage; encouraging Arab and international organizations to carry out archaeological surveys. The department has various maintenance and repair projects, as well as plans for ongoing and ad hoc excavations. One of its projects concerns the National Museum in Amman and the preparation of the necessary equipment for the museum.

In the field of Islamic endowments and religious affairs, the plan aimed to provide sufficient mosques, to maintain them and to develop their work so that they can be intellectual beacons with a real impact on development, and on deepening spiritual, intellectual and moral values. The plan is also concerned with historical and political archives and with Islamic manuscripts, and with the care of these documents; with disseminating Islamic culture among the different sections of society and with supporting the libraries of mosques and establishing a general library in the ministry.

The Royal Scientific Society, founded in 1970, has already completed the preparatory stage of its activities, and has published practical booklets dealing with technical training. It has also founded a library specializing in science, technology and economic development, containing about 30,000 books and 335 university theses. The Five-year Plan entrusted the society with other organizational measures, including the establishment of a national centre for demographic information; the development of an economic information bank; co-ordination with the National Planning Council and the Central Bank in selecting subjects for applied research in

TABLE 1.                Expenditure (in dinars) on economic, social
                        and cultural projects by ministries for 1978 and 1979
                        compared with 1975

| Ministry/department/organization | 1975 | 1978 | 1979 |
|---|---|---|---|
| Ministry of Culture and Youth | — | 75 000 | 100 000 |
| Department of Culture and Arts | 129 000 | 242 000 | 270 000 |
| Directorate of Libraries | — | 137 000 | 175 000 |
| Youth Welfare Organization | 790 000 | 1 110 000 | 1 294 000 |
| Ministry of Education and Instruction | 15 860 576 | 28 594 000 | 35 766 000 |
| Ministry of Information | 345 000 | 487 000 | 543 000 |
| Radio service | 943 626 | 1 020 000 | 1 312 000 |
| Television service | 2 129 910 | 2 787 000 | 3 704 000 |
| Printed material and publishing | 36 000 | 46 000 | 52 000 |
| News agency | 200 000 | 200 000 | 230 000 |
| Ministry of Tourism and Antiquities | | | |
| Tourism | 352 000 | 403 000 | 528 000 |
| Antiquities | 290 085 | 524 000 | 620 000 |
| Ministry of Islamic Endowments and Religious Affairs | 1 550 000 | 1 820 000 | 2 615 000 |
| University of Jordan | 3 522 313 | 9 757 472 | 12 493 865 |
| Princess Hayya Centre | | 75 000 | 88 000 |
| TOTAL | 26 118 410 | 47 277 472 | 59 790 865 |

economic fields; the translation from English of selected educational projects to serve as new reference sources in these fields.

The Jordanian state has provided the necessary funds to achieve the aims of this comprehensive development plan and enable the various ministries, departments and organizations concerned to carry out their economic, social and cultural projects. Table 1 shows the magnitude of the work of cultural development which Jordan has begun to implement.

These statistics show that the Jordanian state in 1978 allocated to cultural affairs the sum of 47,277,472 dinars, or 12 per cent of the state budget, which in that year totalled 371 million dinars. This proportion fell to 11.63 per cent in 1979 when the state allocated to cultural affairs the sum of 59,790,865 dinars out of a total state budget of 513,683,000 dinars. This amount was distributed among the ministries, departments and organizations shown in Table 1. It has not been possible to obtain the budgets of some organizations such as the University of Yarmouk because they are still being constructed and equipped.

It can be seen that the overall rate is beginning to rise; in the course of the next three years it is likely to increase still further until it accounts for as much as 15 per cent of the total state budget. It can also be observed that the Ministry of Education and Instruction and the University of

TABLE 2.          Percentage distribution of amount allocated
                  by the state for education and culture

| Ministry or organization | Percentage |
| --- | --- |
| Ministry of Culture and Youth | 3.18 |
| Ministry of Education and Instruction | 59.9 |
| Ministry of Information | 9.8 |
| Ministry of Tourism and Antiquities | 1.1 |
| Ministry of Islamic Endowments and Religious Affairs | 4.1 |
| University of Jordan | 20.9 |
| Princess Hayya Cultural Centre | 0.14 |
| TOTAL | 99.04 |

Jordan between them account for something like 81 per cent of the total amount allocated by the state for education and culture, in contrast to the Ministry of Culture and Youth, with just over 3 per cent. Table 2 gives the percentages for each of the various Ministries and organizations.

There can be no doubt that the concern of the state for culture and education will be reflected in overall development strategy and will bring about radical changes.

Within the organizational framework of culture and education, especially following the establishment of a ministry specializing in cultural affairs, culture has become the subject of comprehensive planning, with the Jordanian citizen as the focus of all the ministry's endeavours.

# Organizations responsible for cultural affairs

## The Ministry of Culture and Youth

The ministry was formed in accordance with Statute No. 1 of 1977, issued pursuant to article 120 of the Jordanian constitution, by grouping together the Department of Culture and Arts, the Directorate of Libraries and National Archives, and the Youth Welfare Organization.

### THE DEPARTMENT OF CULTURE AND ARTS

The Department of Culture and Arts was founded in 1966 to deal with every aspect of cultural and artistic affairs in the kingdom, and to co-operate with and support the activities of writers, educationalists and artists. The department was originally linked to the Ministry of Culture and Information, which had been entrusted since its creation in 1964 with responsibility for handling cultural and informational affairs, presenting news, pictures and announcements, and publicizing the progress, prosperity and economic and cultural achievements of Jordan. Until it was linked to the Ministry of Culture and Youth, the department was made up of: (a) a culture section; (b) an institute of music; (c) a dramatic-arts section; (d) a popular-arts group; (e) a folklore section; and (f) a plastic-arts section.

The department was involved in the dissemination of books written or translated by Jordanian writers, in the context of the Statute on the Publication and Dissemination of Cultural Production in Jordan, No. 29, issued on 1 June 1969. Before the establishment of the Ministry of Culture and Youth, the Department had published twenty-eight books, i.e. 5.7 per cent of all material published on all subjects over a period of ten years. The publications included information about Jordan and Palestine in particular, and the Arab countries in general.

The Institute of Music, established in 1966, was entrusted with the task of musical education, from both the practical and the theoretical points of

22

view. In addition to its main section it also has a section for special events and one for amateur musicians.

The dramatic-arts section has encouraged and developed dramatic art by popularizing drama throughout society. The Jordanian Theatre Group has presented a number of plays in Jordan, Damascus and Baghdad. This section has trained amateur actors and developed their talents. It has also encouraged the dramatic profession, and encouraged Jordanian writers to write plays on local subjects.

The Popular Arts Group, which was separated from the department when the Ministry of Culture and Youth was established, has worked to invigorate and develop the popular heritage, especially in the field of traditional group dancing. The group comprised twenty-five members, and presented its work in Jordan and in various other Arab and non-Arab countries, winning a number of medals.

The folklore section worked from the middle of 1968 on collecting samples illustrating popular traditions. These samples took the form of clothes, some of the tools used in daily life in rural areas, popular songs and the sayings and recollections of elderly people, Bedouin and popular poetry, etc. The plastic-arts section co-operated with Jordanian artists in holding arts exhibitions, especially of the plastic arts.

The special collection in the care of the department comprised more than 175 pictures by Jordanian artists.

When the Department of Culture and Arts was incorporated in the Ministry of Culture and Youth, it was reorganized in the following five sections (in addition to the normal administrative sections): (a) section for the dissemination and distribution of cultural production; (b) popular traditions section; (c) drama section; (d) periodicals section; (e) Institute of Music and the Fine Arts.

Statute No. 38 of 1977 concerning the dissemination and distribution of cultural production, issued on the basis of article 114 of the Jordanian Constitution, superseded the previous statute on the same subject issued in 1969. In accordance with this new statute, each Jordanian writer must offer to the Department of Culture three copies of the work he intends to have printed. A committee made up of three people is responsible for examining and studying the work, and subsequently making recommendations to the minister. If the work is a translation, the translator is required to obtain prior permission from the publisher or author. The minister decides the value of the cash remuneration for each book, up to a maximum of 1,000 dinars. Remuneration is on the following basis: (a) books in Category A, 1,000 dinars; (b) books in Category B, 600 dinars; (c) books in Category C, 300 dinars.

The popular traditions section, after the establishment of the ministry which endorsed the project, set about surveying the East bank and recording aspects of Jordanian popular life. This section was able, in one year, to make approximately 1,400 hours of cassette recordings embracing

23

numerous topics connected with beliefs, customs, traditions, folklore, medicine, literature, traditional crafts, music and dance. The recordings are now being studied by the researchers and authorities concerned.

The drama section has recently done conspicuous work, especially after the Minister for Culture and Youth decided to form a committee for the theatre sector, which was entrusted with the task of formulating a general policy for drama in its various dimensions and of discussing programmes, selecting theatrical works and identifying the needs of the community in that regard. The periodicals section has been entrusted with publishing three monthly magazines, entitled respectively *Ideas, Youth* and *Arts*. The first of these, a general cultural magazine, started publication in 1966. The second is concerned with youth affairs, and commenced publication in 1968. The third is a specialized arts magazine which started publication in 1978, replacing the popular arts magazine of which thirteen numbers had been published.

Finally, we must mention the Institute of Music and the Fine Arts, which has developed its programmes in a radical form, in accordance with the plans of the Ministry of Culture and Youth. The ministry works to popularize musical and artistic culture among the Jordanian public, and to give children, young people and adults the chance to learn about this kind of culture by means of free training and instruction. Work on this plan began with effect from the start of the 1978/79 academic year.

### THE DIRECTORATE OF LIBRARIES AND NATIONAL ARCHIVES

Statute No. 27 of 1977, (which superseded No. 85 of 1975) provided for the establishment of a Directorate of Libraries and National Archives, attached to the Ministry of Culture and Youth. The Statute defined a literary work as any kind of text (including books, periodicals, newspapers, pamphlets, etc.). It defined a document as any written paper or book, photographic or photostatic picture, cinematic film, microfilm or microfiche, sound or video recording, any drawing, map, or any material involving activity which relates to the concerns and activities of the directorate, provided it was: (a) composed in the course of work undertaken by the state or its agencies; (b) sent to any government office or came within the scope of the work of such an office; (c) was preserved by any public office because of its contents; (d) clarifies the work of any government or official department or is connected with that work; (e) is registered among the contents of the Directorate as having been judged to relate to national affairs.

To enable it to achieve its aims and objectives, the directorate was entrusted with powers and responsibilities enabling it to establish, administer and develop the National Library; set up and administer sections concerned with records, archives and documentation; prepare and develop information, indexes and bibliographies; supervise public libraries and be responsible for co-ordination with and between them, and propose the technical principles for their administration; formulate and apply norms and standards concerning libraries and archives; take on the role of a general and principal centre for all archives and written works; stimulate the heritage and co-ordinate and co-operate with the individual libraries.

The statute entrusted the minister with the task of drafting general policy for the directorate and of supervising the implementation of that policy and of composing directives on the administration of the lending of material and the use of the services of the directorate. It entrusted the Council of Ministers with defining the modalities of presenting documents to the directorate, and the period after which such documents would be available for consultation by specialists and researchers, subject to the approval of the minister. It required ministries, departments, organizations and public departments to provide the directorate with the documents and reports which it requests, and to destroy their records according to the instructions of the directorate. It also required ministries, departments, and public and private organizations to deposit free of charge, a copy of each work published in the kingdom.

### THE YOUTH WELFARE ORGANIZATION

The Youth Welfare Organization has been in operation since 16 October 1966, in accordance with Provisional Law No. 70 of 1966 and Law No. 13 of 1968. The aim of this organization has been to concern itself directly with young people, so as to provide a suitable climate for the development of their talents, aptitudes and skills; to enable them to make profitable use of their time by participating in social, economic and cultural development; and by providing them with opportunities for sound physical and educational development, to equip them to confront the challenges of modern technological society.

Since its establishment, this organization has familiarized itself with the problems encountered by Jordanian youth in their cultural, social and sporting activities by means of direct contact and dealings with young people. It has worked continuously to satisfy the need felt by young people to utilize their capacities to the full in a way that reflects positively on them and on the society in which they live.

The organization has also made it its business to develop leisure facilities for young people, and has so far established twenty-five centres spread throughout the kingdom, catering for a wide variety of activities. Vocational training programmes were introduced in five of these centres during the period of implementation of the 1973–75 Three-year Development Plan. The organization continued to support and encourage the establishment of sporting, social and cultural clubs, and to provide them with technical expertise. This was in addition to the organization's close concern with the Scout and Guide movements and with work camps, youth hostels, sports federations, and exchanges of visits between young people from Jordan and the rest of the Arab world.

In the 1976–80 Five-year Development Plan, the Organization stated that it would create the conditions and means for laying the foundations of sound social development, so as to produce for Jordanian society a pattern of balance between the modern and the traditional; to confront the numerous negative attitudes and superficial concepts, which are by their very nature a manifestation of cultural and social backwardness and which must be changed by a determined effort if society is to be transformed; to strengthen the spiritual development of young people and imbue them with a feeling of pride in their country and in its culture, integrity, heritage and values; to provide a suitable cultural climate for Jordanian young people, and to work on expanding the foundations and scope of action of cultural sources, the eventual aim being to construct a cultural framework characterized by the capacity for discrimination, so that there is no place left for cultures alien to the character of the community; to provide Jordanian young people with an upbringing conducive to their spiritual, physical, intellectual, psychological and social development; to support social and economic development operations; to develop and encourage all forms of sporting activity.

The organization will continue to establish youth centres in towns and villages, and to set up cultural clubs and programmes in co-operation with the Ministry of Culture and Youth (Department of Culture and Arts). Since the creation of the ministry, the organization has already, in co-operation with the Department of Culture and Arts, organized a complete cultural season with drama, seminars, musical events, poetry evenings, lectures on history and exhibitions of books, paintings, etc. These activities have been made accessible throughout the kingdom by means of the youth centres, which are distributed all over Jordan, so as to develop the general cultural resources available to citizens and to provide facilities to assist with basic cultural education which is necessary for progress in all the various spare-time activities.

The Hussein Youth Centre was founded in the middle of 1968 to provide a suitable meeting place and climate for Jordanian youth. It was created to implement the King's desire to give every possible encouragement to young people of exceptional creative ability and initiative. It had been called the Hussein Sports Centre, but, in view of the fact that it provides general facilities not restricted to sports, it was re-named the Hussein Youth Centre in 1969. This centre comprises: (a) the International Stadium of Amman, which holds up to 30,000 spectators; (b) the cultural centre, which is used as a main hall for congresses and for musical and dramatic events, entertainments, etc., and which holds up to 3,000 spectators; (c) sports grounds of various kinds, a club, a hotel and a restaurant.

Since its establishment, the Ministry of Culture and Youth has worked energetically to spread knowledge and culture, to stimulate and disseminate the heritage, to encourage and sponsor talent, and to support writing, translation and publication, etc.

Its activities began with the holding of the first conference of Arab Ministers of Culture on 20 December 1976, in which delegates from all Arab countries participated for a period of four days, together with Unesco and the Director-General and Deputy Director-General of ALECSO. Following the conference, the 'Amman Declaration' was issued, which came to be a comprehensive charter for the Arab cultural movement. In this declaration, it was stated that the Arab community intends to put an end to all traces of cultural deprivation and overt or covert intellectual aggression. The participants also proclaimed the importance of supporting the development of the international cultural role of the Arab community, for the good of humanity, and of the recovery of areas of human culture taken over by colonialism during the past centuries; the need to draw up a unified Arab cultural policy as a means of cultural development, and as a support for a general plan for comprehensive development; the need to achieve integration and co-ordination between the work of educational systems and information media in the Arab countries, so as to increase the effectiveness of cultural work and to expand the scope of cultural services for the people; the importance of affirming that culture is a right for all people, analogous to their right to education and their political and social rights; the need for an effort to spread the use of Arabic as the language of education at all levels and of all kinds, as well as in scientific research and in the information and culture media, on the basis that the national language is the most important form of propaganda for unity, and is the correct way to call for an authentic culture for the Arab community. Finally, the declaration stated the desire of the Arab community for its various governments and administrations to co-operate to achieve the contents of the declaration and the recommendations of the conference by means of programmes and definite projects to be carried out by ALECSO in accordance with a long-term plan.

The Amman Declaration also confirmed the importance of the steps taken and the studies carried out by ALECSO with a view to the creation within that organization of an Arab fund for cultural development and the need to form a standing committee for Arab culture, that would be responsible *inter alia* for monitoring the implementation of the recommendations of the Conference of Ministers and preparing for subsequent conferences.

Only a few days after the publication of this declaration, the ministry began to implement its recommendations. With effect from the beginning of 1977, the ministry founded the first League of Plastic Artists, formally registered with the Youth Welfare Organization as No. 170. The first working meeting was also held between the Minister for Culture and Youth and Jordanian artists. During this meeting, the minister listened to a presentation of the state of the plastic arts in Jordan, and to the suggestions of the artists regarding ways in which their activities might be encouraged. The minister spoke about the ministry's new plan for creating a suitable environment for artists, and about its readiness to support and encourage the artistic movement in Jordan. The first working meeting was also held between the Minister for Culture and Jordanian writers, during which the minister listened to the writers' points of view and their requests. Discussion ranged over many subjects, including cultural production and dissemination, music, cinema, popular traditions and the periodicals published by the ministry.

In view of the Jordanian state's desire to encourage cultural production, a Statute, No. 19, was promulgated in April 1977 concerning state prizes to be awarded in recognition of achievement in literature and art. At the end of that year, which the country celebrated as a jubilee year on the occasion of the twenty-fifth anniversary of His Majesty King Hussein's assumption of his constitutional powers, monetary awards and prizes were awarded to three writers and one artist. His Majesty also distributed royal diplomas to eight holders of the Silver Jubilee Certificate awarded in recognition of their contributions to the cultural life of the kingdom during the past twenty-five years.

The same year saw the promulgation of the Statute concerning the Directorate of Libraries and National Archives and the Statute concerning the Dissemination and Distribution of Cultural Production. The Ministry gave material and moral encouragement to the Association of Jordanian Libraries and the Jordanian Book League, and to other associations and leagues. It also participated in the conference of the Council of the Federation of Arab Universities, and in the Damascus Festival of Dramatic Arts; in the seminar on copyright held in Rabat in May 1977; in the conference of Arab writers held in Tripoli (Libyan Arab Jamahiriya); and in the second Arab book fair held in Doha in December 1977.

In the field of dissemination of cultural production, the ministry published a group of works of fiction and works of research, together with an illustrated book, on the great Arab revolt. A number of popular songs were recorded and the record distributed by an international orchestra group with the aim of popularizing Jordanian music. The distributor of the music and leader of the orchestra was the musician Yusef Khasho.

In the field of the plastic arts, the ministry lent its support to exhibitions of the works of Jordanian and other Arab artists as well as to exhibitions presented in accordance with cultural agreements. Perhaps the most important exhibition held in that year was the first Fine Arts Exhibition, which brought together paintings representing all artistic tendencies. Arab and international musical events were also organized. Foreign-film weeks were held. In the field of the theatre, a plan was drawn up to establish a drama school to train Jordanian actors, preliminary steps were taken with a view to the establishment of a league of Jordanian dramatists, and a drama committee was formed to draw up a general policy for the drama movement. The theatre season turned out to be rich in creative ability. A periodicals committee was formed to supervise the publication of intellectual, artistic and youth magazines. From the time of its creation, the ministry has been active in studying the cultural agreements concluded between Jordan and Arab and foreign states, so as to make it possible to draw up a working programme giving the time-frame for implementation of their provisions, especially in so far as they relate to art, culture and youth. The agreements call for the exchange of information, printed material, archives, manuscripts, historical documents, catalogues, periodicals, audio-visual material, cultural films, books and other publications. They also call for co-operation in the fields of literature and drama, cinema, music and the plastic arts, by means of exchanges of visits and invitations between writers, artists, authors and persons engaged in artistic activity, and by establishing and exchanging exhibitions. They call for the exchange of drama groups, the holding of concerts, artistic and performing-arts festivals, and appearances by popular-arts groups; the holding of seminars and lectures and the exchange of cultural films, in particular; for the dissemination of cultural production and printed works, cinema films, records and tapes, the organization of study missions or educational courses in the spheres of culture and art; the establishment of libraries or the opening of special wings in non-specialist libraries to house information about the country with which the agreement was signed.

It is worth noting that twenty-three agreements have been signed in this field, and other agreements have been prepared for signature. Early in 1978, the ministry started to implement further cultural programmes in the various youth centres. The aim was to encourage the spread of cultural activities throughout the towns and villages of Jordan by means of these centres and in co-operation with the Department of Culture and Arts. Artistic exhibitions and exhibitions of books were held, together with poetry and music evenings, public lectures and performances of plays. The ministry published more books. In the field of the plastic arts, seventeen exhibitions were held of the works of Jordanian, Arab and international artists. Additional cultural agreements were signed. The ministry invited a number of famous international groups to appear in concerts, revues, etc., both in Amman and elsewhere in Jordan. A start was made by the theatre section in the Department of Culture and Arts on implementing the training programme for producers. The first League of Jordanian Dramatists was established. The Drama Committee began to draw up a general policy for the theatre movement, by formulating general principles, discussing programmes, and selecting appropriate dramatic works. As a result, nine local, Arab and international plays were presented and taken on tour in towns and villages throughout the kingdom. These endeavours culminated in the holding, in July 1978, of a seminar, the first of its kind, for those involved in the various branches of theatrical activity.

In the sphere of dissemination of cultural production, books were published on the political and social history of Jordan, together with collections of poetry and a book of popular proverbs. The ministry participated in the third Book Fair in Kuwait, and in the Standing Committee on Arab Culture which discussed the subjects to be examined by the second Conference of Arab Ministers of Culture. The ministry also announced the award of state prizes for achievement in historical research, poetry and the plastic arts. The second Exhibition of Fine Arts was held, at which 160 paintings by fifty-two artists were displayed.

In the field of popular traditions, a start was made on the establishment of a reference archive of popular traditions, to be based on tape recordings made in the course of a comprehensive survey of the entire kingdom. Several hundred tapes have already been recorded under this scheme.

The ministry intends to produce a documentary film about the great Arab revolt, and a book on the history of Jordan from the earliest times, as well as a book to be entitled *Twenty-five Years of Cultural Life in Jordan*. The ministry will also increase the number of books it produces, and will start to publish the magazines *Ideas* and *Arts* on a regular monthly basis. It will implement the projects for a National Library, a Faculty of Fine Arts in the University of Jordan, a National Museum, and a plan for the Royal Theatre, which will deservedly rank as the outstanding cultural achievement of this period.

The declared aims of the Ministry of Culture and Youth are set out in the speech which the minister delivered in the National Consultative Assembly in 1978. In this speech, he stated that culture, in the view of the ministry, consists in fostering the intellectual and social heritage which forms the character of the people or community, especially as regards creative innovation and aesthetic expression in the widest sense, as embodied in such activities as literature, poetry, the graphic arts, sculpture, music, architecture, acting, etc., and in developing and enriching the inherited social fabric by drawing on the ideas and artistic achievements of the whole world. In this context, he went on to say that the work of the ministry must be directed to the following aims:

Revitalization of the heritage which has contributed to the creation of our national identity and of our Arab community, by associating the best of what has been handed down to us from our heritage with our efforts to create the future of the nation.

Encouragement of the intellectual movement in Jordan, so that it can contribute to the interaction which advances our distinctive identity and our participation in the progress of our Arab nation and of the world. Special encouragement of the universal idea of enlightenment, connected with the hopes of our nation and community and requiring constructive work and a positive attitude.

Encouragement of the artistic movement in the graphic arts, sculpture, the theatre and music, so as to enable these arts to perform their task of stimulating taste and elevating the spirit and helping to construct Jordan in a manner consistent with the highest standards of culture and civilization.

Promotion of creative artistic and intellectual activity on the part of individuals and organizations, and encouragement of general aesthetic awareness in all its aspects.

The minister observed that the incorporation of youth welfare activities in the same ministry as culture and the arts, gave a clear indication of its confidence in young people, and of its belief that their development can best proceed side by side with cultural progress, so that they are a source of inspiration and the object of intellectual, psychological and medical care from the earliest age, protected by the true values of the nation as well as being the heirs of its spiritual and intellectual heritage at the time when they are developing the capacity for interrelation, creation and progress.

## The Ministry of Education and Instruction

Anyone who follows the development of education and instruction in Jordan will find that the educational awakening achieved by Jordan in the last quarter of a century is one of the country's most important cultural achievements. This awakening may be traced back to the determination of His Majesty King Hussein, and his total dedication to the service of his country and its development. Despite the political and economic problems to which the country has been exposed during this period, Jordan has been able, under the leadership of its young king, to produce pioneering achievements that scarcely any country with similar possibilities could have attained in such a short time. If Jordan is poor in natural and economic resources, God has endowed it with human riches which have been the principal source of its development and progress. For this reason the Ministry of Education and Instruction is determined that the young people of Jordan shall receive the best possible leadership and guidance, and an education which, while taking due account of recent educational trends and systems throughout the world, is at the same time fully in accordance with the highest ideals of our community and firmly grounded in our ancient heritage and lofty moral values.

Since its creation, Jordan has been aware of its great responsibility towards its sister Arab states, and has participated effectively in their development and march towards prosperity by providing them with an enormous number of workers, trained personnel and highly qualified specialists. These people naturally tend to return to their own country, bringing with them money estimated at half Jordan's national income.

Education and instruction in general are affected by political, social and economic conditions. This influence has also been evident in the

31

Hashemite Kingdom of Jordan. In the period of the Mandate, the aim of education was to provide clerical workers for the government system. The education budget in 1921 was £6,000 sterling. In 1936 there was an improvement following the publication of Education Statute, No. 2 of 1939, by which an educational administration was created in Jordan with the task of establishing, administering and generally supervising state schools, encouraging scientific and literary movements, the Scout movement and sports in schools, and promoting the fine arts and supervising general culture and public morals.

In this statute, compulsory education appeared for the first time. Four years' schooling was given in rural areas and five years in the towns.

In the period of independence, the state began to guarantee education for its citizens without distinction, within the limits of its capacities, as stipulated in the amended Constitution of 1952. Compulsory education now included the entire primary phase, and continued for seven years until it was changed to six years from the start of the 1954/55 academic year.

In 1955, Education Law No. 2 was issued, defining the principal tasks of the Ministry of Education. Article 3 stated that the fundamental task of the ministry was to make instruction available to the people, and to form the character of the citizen; to bring up a physically healthy young generation with a sound set of beliefs, ideas and principles, conscious of their duty towards God and the nation, and eager to work for the good of the country; to supervise the various schools and centres.

Education made considerable progress in the 1950s, because people were becoming aware of it and were taking an interest in it. It was also because of the measures taken by the state to stimulate education, in the firm belief that education is a form of investment which contributes to social and economic progress.

This educational development led eventually to the promulgation of Law No. 16 of 1964 concerning education and instruction, which set out for the first time a clearly defined philosophy for education in Jordan. This philosophy derived its principles from the Jordanian Constitution, the situation of the country, its experience and values, and its ideals. The new law laid down aims for Jordanian education, and these aims have since formed the basis of the country's academic curricula. They are: (a) to guarantee for Jordanian and Arab society that the coming generations will believe in God and in their own identity and ideals as members of the Arab nation; (b) to educate God-fearing citizens who are loyal to king and country; (c) to promote understanding of the environment in its natural, social and cultural aspects; (d) to foster the acquisition of basic skills; and (e) to help the individual to achieve a balanced physical, intellectual, social and emotional development so that he can become an exemplary member of society.

With this law, Jordan took a pioneering step by making the period of compulsory education nine years, made up of a six-year cycle of primary education and a preparatory cycle of three years. As a result of this law, the compulsory cycle took in a proportion of 75.7 per cent of children of all ages in the year 1966/67. In 1966/70, it covered 91 per cent of this category, and in 1975/76 it covered 94.3 per cent. During the past twenty-five years, the number of pupils in the various stages of education has multiplied many times. While the number of students of either sex on both banks of the kingdom in 1951/52 totalled 139,670, in 1975/76 it totalled 577,466. As a rule, an increase in the number of pupils is followed by an increase in the number of schools, teachers and educational services. Between 1951/52 and 1975/76 the number of schools rose from 449 to 2,356.

The number of teachers rose from 2,041 in 1951/52 to 16,826 in 1975/76. The responsibilities of the Ministry of Education and Instruction, as the principal educational authority in the kingdom, increased by approximately the same proportion. Whereas in 1951/52, the amount allocated to education totalled 3,089,400 dinars (2.1 per cent of the state budget) in 1975/76 it totalled 18,610,550 dinars, or 7.3 per cent of the state budget.

In the field of educational services, the Ministry of Education and Instruction took on responsibility for the printing and distribution of all kinds of school textbooks free of charge, establishing a section for school books and curricula in 1963. A higher committee was formed which subsequently became the Higher Council for Education and Instruction, with responsibility for studying, approving and implementing plans for textbooks as well as for formulating educational policy in Jordan.

As well as the section for school textbooks, the ministry established others to improve such areas of education as teaching aids, educational supervision, educational television, broadcasting for schools, school libraries, psychological and social guidance, school laboratories, educational documentation and research, teacher-training, etc.

The ministry also opened new single-sex schools in remote rural areas and in Bedouin encampments, but had to authorize co-educational schools in places where there were not sufficient boys or girls to justify separate establishments. It also established joint classes in places where the number of pupils in each class was not sufficient to require a separate classroom. The ministry encouraged the education of girls, which had fallen seriously behind that of boys. In 1951/52, male pupils outnumbered female pupils by three to one, but in 1975/76 enrolments for the two sexes were very nearly equal.

To ensure that there were suitable school buildings, the ministry took over a large amount of the necessary land, and established new schools in various towns and villages in the kingdom. It is continuing to implement this policy despite the high cost involved.

There is no more effective instrument of economic, social and cultural advancement than education, and the Ministry of Education and Instruction has accordingly continued to expand, diversify and improve it. Whereas in 1953/54 secondary education began after the seventh year of

33

primary education and lasted for four years, its duration was extended to five years in 1954/55, and changed to three years in 1961/62, following the separation of the preparatory level from the secondary level in 1957/58.

With effect from 1961/62, the secondary level was split into a 'science side' and an 'arts side'. It was subsequently further divided, with the introduction of specialized secondary courses in industry and agriculture, and more recently in commerce, home economics, etc., for women, nursing and postal communications.

Mindful of the importance of linking education with development, the Ministry of Education and Instruction endeavours to take account in its educational planning of the need for an adequate supply of qualified manpower to implement the nation's economic and social development programmes as rapidly as possible. It has also taken steps to implement all the educational projects contained in these programmes, beginning with the five-year economic development programme of 1962/67, and continuing with the three-year and five-year development plans that followed.

The Ministry of Education and Instruction was able to strengthen its educational links with Arab and other friendly countries during this time. It also drew on the results of experiments and research carried out in the various countries of the world, as well as on studies and reports received from international and regional organizations; all this helped it to undertake educational projects which were of pioneering significance not only in the Arab world but internationally.

In 1976, two comprehensive secondary schools were opened in Amman, one for boys and one for girls, together with a vocational school for girls. The same year saw the opening of a specialized engineering institute (polytechnic) which will help to keep the labour market supplied with technicians and assistant engineers in the fields of electrical, civil, chemical, mechanical and construction engineering, as well as training vocational instructors.

In addition, the Five-year Development Plan for 1976/80 contained a number of educational projects aimed at providing the qualified technical and other personnel required for economic development.

In the field of higher education, Jordan has made rapid advances. There was no higher education in the country in 1950/51, except for a one-year vocational course in agriculture at the Khadura School and a one-year teacher-training course. By the end of the 1950s however, two-year courses were available at teacher-training institutes or at the al-Jabiha Institute of Agriculture. There was also a one-year course in Islamic Law as well as training courses for vocational instructors at the Amman School of Industry the Khadura School of Agriculture and the freshmen's class in Bir Zeit. During the 1960s, higher educational facilities were further expanded and diversified; by the end of the decade they included ten teacher-training centres offering two-year courses at the post-secondary level. In 1962/63, the University of Jordan was founded. The first faculty to be established was that of Literature. This was followed by faculties of Islamic Law

(1964/65), Sciences (1965/66), Business and Economics, Education, Engineering, Agriculture, Medicine, and, most recently, Civil Law.

In 1976/77, the University of Yarmouk was opened in a temporary building in the city of Irbid, It is expected that this university will expand as planned until enrolments (both sexes) total as many as 25,000. Since their foundation, the two universities have been regarded as outstanding features of the Jordanian awakening under His Majesty King Hussein.

## EDUCATIONAL PHILOSOPHY

In the Hashemite Kingdom of Jordan, educational philosophy derives from the Jordanian Constitution. This philosophy finds expression in faith in God and the high ideals of the Arab community, and in the unity, freedom and identity of that community in the united and integral Arab nation on the basis that Jordan is an Arab state, that its system of government is a representative hereditary monarchical system, and that the Jordanian people are part of the Arab community. This philosophy also finds expression in its affirmation of the Arab character of Palestinian occupied territory and the lands seized from the Arab nation, and of the importance of working to recover these lands.

This philosophy proclaims the need to respect both the integrity and freedom of the individual and the general interest of society, and to ensure that neither takes precedence over the other. It also stresses the importance of social justice and of providing equal educational opportunities for all citizens of either sex in accordance with their individual capabilities, and of helping every student to achieve harmonious physical, intellectual, social and emotional development, so that he or she can become a self-reliant responsible member of society. It likewise emphasizes the contribution that education can make to the overall development of Jordanian society in the context of an integrated Arab nation: (a) by improving the natural environment through industrialization and control of natural resources; (b) by promoting the development and exploitation of technology, while at the same time paying careful attention to its increasing influence and to the problems it can generate, with a view to anticipating these problems and finding solutions to those that cannot be avoided; and (c) by fusing together the different population groups into a harmonious and cohesive Arab Jordanian society, through pride in Arab values and spiritual ideals, and the fostering of sound social traditions in a manner consistent with continuous cultural development.

The philosophy in question also stresses the importance of respect for freedom and the democratic system, which permits citizens to take part in self-government and the administration of their affairs in various fields, on the basis of knowledge, common interest and positive participation in the cultural development of the world as represented in the sciences, arts and literature.

### THE GENERAL AIMS OF THE MINISTRY
### OF EDUCATION AND INSTRUCTION

The general aims of education in Jordan derive from the above philosophy of education and are as follows:

1. The preparation of good citizens, believing in: (a) the fundamental elements on which the philosophy of education in Jordan is based; (b) the full rights of citizenship, and the responsibilities resulting from those rights; (c) the implementation of ethical standards in all fields of individual and social conduct; (d) enterprise and perseverance in work; a positive spirit in behaviour; effective co-operation with others; adherence to the democratic method in human relations.

2. The promotion of understanding of the environment in its natural, social and cultural aspects, starting with the home and gradually widening the pupil's grasp of this concept to embrace the school, the village, the town, the province, Jordan, the Arab nation and human society as a whole. This involves inculcating in him an analytical grasp of all aspects of the environment, its different problems and its present and anticipated needs, and a positive awareness of the duty to participate in the development of the environment within the limits of his training and capacity.

3. The development of the following basic skills and habits: (a) easy transmission of ideas to other people by oral expression in classical Arabic; (b) easy transmission of ideas to other people by written expression in classical Arabic; (c) familiarity with everyday mathematical operations; (d) close and discerning attention to what other people are saying and doing, so as to benefit from their views and experience; (e) use of the scientific method in research, in thinking, in forming conclusions and in distinguishing between true and false information; (f) objectivity in criticism, based on a constructive, helpful and progressive approach; (g) the acquisition and constant development of the habit of reading for enjoyment and for increasing one's store of knowledge.

4. Helping the individual towards harmonious physical, intellectual, social and emotional development, while respecting the differences between individuals; developing creativity among the talented, and providing an opportunity for the less gifted in their various ways to develop within the limits of their abilities thereby satisfying individual needs while at the same time promoting the development of society in its different aspects.

5. Raising the level of individual and community health by disseminating correct information and developing good habits of behaviour and work.

6. Raising the level of individual and community leisure activities by promoting healthy recreational habits and by developing various forms of Jordanian and Arab popular art.

7. Raising the economic level of the individual and of the community and increasing the national income through the provision of equal educational opportunities for all—an aim which implies the diversification of educational programmes so that, on the one hand, they accord with the wishes and inclinations of individuals, and, on the other, they satisfy the present and anticipated needs of the country in all spheres within the framework of the state's comprehensive planning.

## THE WORK OF THE MINISTRY OF EDUCATION AND INSTRUCTION

To ensure the attainment of Jordan's general educational objectives within the framework of the nation's educational philosophy, it is necessary for the ministry:

To create and administer government-controlled educational establishments of various types and levels.

To supervise all educational establishments, whether national or foreign, in order to ensure that they contribute to the attainment of Jordan's general educational objectives and that they comply with all the provisions of the relevant legislation.

To establish adult-education centres to disseminate general culture to all members of the community thoughout the kingdom.

To strengthen scientific, cultural and artistic links between Jordan and other Arab countries, so as to unite Arab culture throughout the Arab nation.

To encourage and organize a wide variety of activities for young people, both inside and outside educational establishments, including physical education, military training and the Scout movement, camping and travel both within and outside the Arab world, etc.

To encourage scientific and cultural movements by creating libraries and museums; by making appropriate use of radio, television and other information media; by organizing lectures and holding commemorative festivals; by encouraging the creation of clubs and associations; by printing scientific, cultural and artistic magazines; by disseminating the Islamic Arab heritage; by promoting scientific research and publishing the results of this research; and by sponsoring and encouraging creative intellectual and artistic activity through the provision of appropriate incentives.

To encourage popular art and the fine arts in all their respective forms, both inside and outside educational establishments, in accordance with the nation's values and ideals;

To supervise and organize the agencies responsible for arranging the admission of students to foreign universities and for providing services to these students.

UNIVERSITY EDUCATION

## The University of Jordan

The promulgation on 2 September 1962 of the Royal Decree concerning the foundation of the University of Jordan marked the beginning of university education in the kingdom. Laws, statutes and directives were also issued for the guidance and organization of this university, so that it might serve as a pioneering national institution, breaking new ground in different areas of human knowledge. These documents included Provisional Law No. 33 of 1975 and Provisional Law No. 49 of 1976, both amending Law No. 52 of 1972 concerning the University of Jordan.

The creation of the university was the culmination of the general educational awakening in Jordan. The number of pupils and schools had multiplied during the previous ten years, elementary education had become compulsory, and secondary education had diversified, the school-enrolment ratio had risen to a higher level than in other Arab countries, and in some developed countries outside the region, and the number of those completing their secondary studies had considerably increased and could now be counted in thousands. All these reasons impelled the authorities concerned to consider creating a national university.

Consideration had been given to starting this university over a long period of time, especially after the country had finished establishing its basic infrastructure. Every year, both in official and non-official circles, the need for a national Jordanian university was more strongly felt. This trend became more sharply focused at the beginning of the 1950s, when the state began forming committees to study the subject, and invited Arab and foreign experts on numerous occasions to formulate reports and recommendations regarding the creation of the proposed university. These efforts were crowned by the promulgation of the royal decree concerning the foundation of the university, which was immediately put into effect. Less than four months after the promulgation of the decree, first-year instruction began in the faculty of Literature, the first to start work. Barely three years later, on 1 October 1965, two other faculties opened: the faculty of Sciences and the faculty of Economics and Business. The university now has nine faculties.

The number of students accepted in the first year of the university's life was 167, including eighteen female students. There were only eight part-time. The university started with a budget of only 50,000 dinars, and a site of six hectares (presented by the government) on which stood two old buildings, one of which was used for the library and offices for the teaching staff.

Now, eighteen years later, there are 8,203 students, in the university; and more than a third of them are female. The teaching staff numbers 434. Its budget for 1978 amounted to 9,757,472 dinars. The university precincts now cover an area of more than ten hectares, on which there are teaching-rooms, auditoria, offices, residences, a library, etc.

## The aims and objectives of the University of Jordan

Article 5 of the university law stated that the University of Jordan will aim to serve Arab society, and especially Jordanian society, by all possible means, and especially by arranging opportunities for study and specialization in fields of knowledge which meet the needs of the country, whilst being concerned with general culture and concentrating on quality; by carrying out and encouraging scientific research, promoting intellectual independence, personal initiative and a spirit of community-oriented work; by developing in its students a spirit of scientific inquiry; by concerning itself with Arab and Islamic civilization, and disseminating its heritage; by fostering moral values and promoting a sense of patriotism and responsibility; by promoting and developing technology in the service of society; by promoting the advancement of literature and the arts, and encouraging scientific progress; by concerning itself with national and international culture, and developing the national heritage; by strengthening links with Arab and international universities and scientific organizations.

One of the aims of the University of Jordan is that study there should not be limited to providing the student with information contained in any particular book. Instead, it should be a means of developing the student's intellect, building his personality, expanding his general powers of cultural discernment, referring him to different sources in any one subject so that he becomes acquainted with different points of view, familiarizing him with scientific procedures and methods of research, and equipping him to undertake the comparison of texts, narratives and opinions. Another of the university's aims is to achieve a positive and constant interaction between the university and the society around it by creating a general cultural and intellectual climate of which it is the centre. To do this, the university opens its doors to Jordanian writers and scholars, who participate in its public occasions and in seminars which bring together its teaching staff, important Arab scholars and writers, and foreign Arabists who are invited by the university to give lectures and hold seminars. The university also makes its theatre available to Jordanian, Arab and foreign musical and drama groups, whose performances are attended by large numbers of citizens belonging to every social class.

It should finally be mentioned that the University of Jordan is considered to be an important new departure in the Arab world, especially as regards its relations with the government, for which there is no precedent in the region. It is the first national university in the Arab world to be completely independent of government, materially, administratively and academically. It is supervised by a council of trustees, made up of eighteen members selected for their experience and judgement. This council supports and safeguards the independence of the university, and does everything

39

# Organizations responsible for cultural affairs

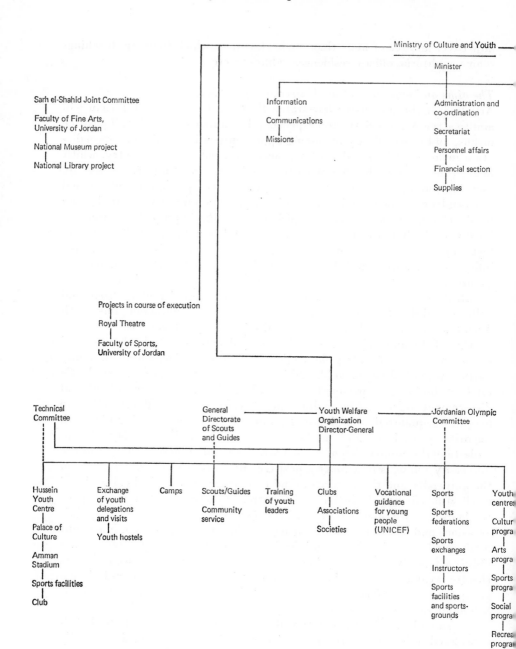

# Organizations responsible for cultural affairs

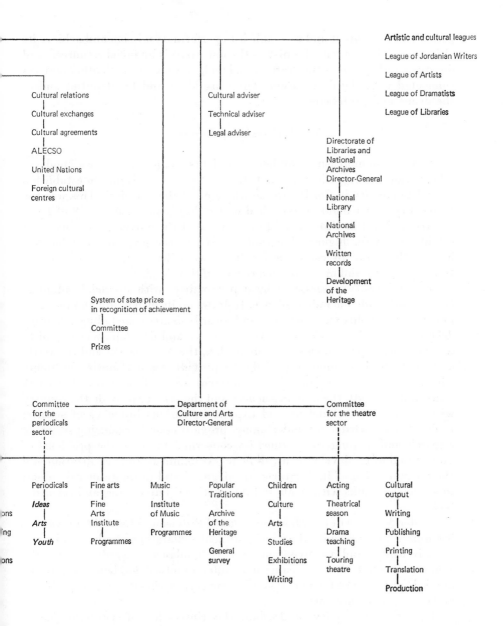

Artistic and cultural leagues

League of Jordanian Writers

League of Artists

League of Dramatists

League of Libraries

Cultural relations

Cultural exchanges

Cultural agreements

ALECSO

United Nations

Foreign cultural centres

Cultural adviser

Technical adviser

Legal adviser

Directorate of Libraries and National Archives Director-General

National Library

National Archives

Written records

Development of the Heritage

System of state prizes in recognition of achievement

Committee

Prizes

Committee for the periodicals sector

Department of Culture and Arts Director-General

Committee for the theatre sector

Periodicals

Ideas

Arts

Youth

Fine arts

Fine Arts Institute

Programmes

Music

Institute of Music

Programmes

Popular Traditions

Archive of the Heritage

General survey

Children

Culture

Arts

Studies

Exhibitions

Writing

Acting

Theatrical season

Drama teaching

Touring theatre

Cultural output

Writing

Publishing

Printing

Translation

Production

41

possible to promote it and to enable it to perform its mission and achieve its objectives. The council administers the university's financial resources, and discusses and approves the draft annual budget, together with other matters connected with the designation of the president and his deputies and of the deans and professors.

## The University of Yarmouk

Because of the increasing number of students completing their secondary-school studies, the authorities had strong reasons for wishing to establish a second university in Jordan to absorb some of the overflow. This was the University of Yarmouk, established under Provisional Law No. 9 of 1976.

Article 3 of this Provisional Law states that the university is a national establishment for higher education, located in the province of Irbid but having the right to establish faculties, scientific centres, research and training centres and institutes in any part of the kingdom.

The university possesses a legal personality, with financial, administrative and academic independence. It draws up its own study and teaching programmes, holds examinations and awards degrees, including honorary degrees. The university's objective is to serve and develop society, and to work for the improvement of life in Jordan, the Arab nation and the world as a whole; to disseminate knowledge by providing opportunities for higher education and for specialization in different areas of the natural sciences (pure and applied), the human sciences and the arts; to provide the country with specialists, technicians and experts in various branches of science; to develop knowledge by undertaking, promoting and organizing scientific research and helping the authorities concerned to solve the problems of society and of its development; to foster Arab and Islamic civilization and the dissemination of its heritage; to safeguard and promote moral values; to strengthen links with Arab and international universities and scientific bodies.

Under Article 6 of the above-mentioned Provisional Law, the university is required to concern itself with the student's character, conduct and sense of citizenship, and to give him positive guidance towards serving the common good. It is also required to offer practical guidance in various applied spheres with the aim of serving society, solving its present problems and obviating future ones.

Like the University of Jordan, the University of Yarmouk has a council of trustees. This council, has eleven members who are Jordanian citizens with the ability, experience and capacity to discharge the responsibilities entrusted to them, and thereby promote the attainment of the university's objectives. Article 10 of the Provisional Law provides that the council of trustees shall be responsible for maintaining the independence of the university, for organizing its financial resources, and for ensuring that the necessary means are available to enable it to attain its objectives; for drawing up its general policy and examining its draft statutes and draft budget; for deciding the university's fees; for examining the annual reports and for dealing with other matters connected with the university, including the designation of the president, whose appointment shall be made by royal decree. It is worth noting that the university began with a faculty of Science and Literature comprising eighteen departments divided into four sections: science, literature, economics and sciences. If we bear in mind that the university opened in 1976/77 in a temporary building in Irbid and that it is ultimately intended to have as many as 25,000 students (male and female), we can appreciate the importance of the role which it is destined to play in higher education. It will share its difficult task with its sister establishment, the University of Jordan.

## The Ministry of Information

The Ministry of Information was created in 1974 to be the official spokesman of the kingdom and, through its various component bodies, to reflect Jordan's activities in all areas. It was known as the Ministry of Culture and Information until the creation of the Ministry of Culture and Youth. After the Department of Culture and Arts had been detached from it and incorporated in the Ministry of Culture and Youth, the Ministry of Culture and Information became known simply as the Ministry of Information. It comprised the Department of Printed Material and Publishing, the Jordanian News Agency, the Radio Service and the Jordanian Television Organization.

The Department of Printed Material and Publishing is the senior department of the ministry in terms of age. It was established in 1946, when the country acquired its independence and became a kingdom rather than an emirate. At first, it was attached to the Foreign Ministry and then to the Prime Minister's Office, where it remained until 1964, when it was incorporated in the Ministry of Culture and Information. Its work had initially been limited to supervision of the press, but it subsequently began to publish a daily bulletin of local news to facilitate the work of journalists and to provide information about the kingdom. The department's first information publication, *The Jordanian Press Guide*, appeared in 1958, as did the magazine *Jordanian Letter*, which was designed to explain the Jordanian point of view and to cover local activities. In 1963, the department began publishing *The Jordanian Year Book*, of which many successive editions appeared. In the same year, the department opened a branch in Jerusalem, which continued to function until 1967, when Jerusalem came under Israeli occupation. The department publishes leaflets, booklets and information pamphlets in Arabic and English, and inspects the printed material coming into the kingdom before it is distributed.

The Jordanian News Agency was established as an independent

43

department in August 1969. It is an information apparatus which collects official and general information about the various activities taking place in Jordan and distributes it to official and other information media, newspaper correspondents and Arab and international news agencies in Jordan. The agency follows and covers news in Jordan, as well as affairs in the Arab world and elsewhere, including information about them in its bulletins.

### THE RADIO SERVICE

Jordan did not have its own independent radio service until the end of April 1948, when Arab officials in the broadcasting service, established in Palestine during the Mandate, seized the opportunity provided by confused conditions in the government system, as a consequence of the ending of the mandate on 15 May 1948, to help Jordanian army personnel to transport to Ramallah all the radio equipment in Jerusalem that could be transported; Ramallah was in the zone defended by the Jordanian army against Israeli occupation. Broadcasting was placed under the authority of the Jordanian Government and of the General Military Governor of Palestine. This state of affairs continued until the two banks of the Jordan were officially united on 24 April 1950; since then the radio service has been known as the Hashemite Kingdom of Jordan Radio.

On 1 September 1956, His Majesty King Hussein opened Radio Amman. On 1 March 1959, he opened the new radio organization 'Amman Calling', the radio service of the Hashemite Kingdom of Jordan. His Majesty opened the new radio studios in Jerusalem on 23 August 1959; Jerusalem Radio stopped broadcasting as a result of the June 1967 war. His Majesty is shortly to announce the start of 'Voice of Jordan', broadcasting at ten times the power of the present service. It will be possible for pupils in schools throughout the kingdom to receive school lessons transmitted directly to their classrooms throughout the day. Citizens unable to enrol in schools will also be able to benefit from these broadcasts.

As soon as the arrangements indicated above have been completed and new studios have been built, the Radio Service will start broadcasting two separate programmes. One of these will be a general programme using the main station. The other will be a local radio programme. For the first time, there will be a radio service broadcasting material of local interest and functioning as a separate operation with its own distinct identity.

The ultimate intention is for the Radio Service to comprise four separate programmes, two in Arabic and two in English.

The Jordanian Radio Service has been considered as a kind of school of popular culture. It exercises its responsibilities towards the people with whom it communicates and whose life it shares. It tries to increase the common store of knowledge, as a public medium of communication responsible for developing the public sense of common identity. Its treatment of issues is designed to reinforce social awareness, responsibility and partici-

44

pation. It trusts in dialogue as a means of creating awareness, and in the transmission of culture with the aim of guiding and educating that awareness.

The Radio Service of the Hashemite Kingdom of Jordan aims to create and stimulate a feeling of national solidarity, on the basis of awareness of the realities of life. The service is a medium for social dialogue between the different classes and intellectual levels of society. It also concerns itself with the heritage of society, with the powers latent in its national aspirations and goals, and with its links with the Arab environment and the whole world.

These objectives and responsibilities have been reflected in the programmes of the Radio Service, which now broadcasts twenty-six cultural programmes each week, representing 11 per cent of all transmissions. These programmes try to clarify the special characteristics of the people and the community, to strengthen values, customs and traditions, and deepen religious belief and patriotism. They express the people's eagerness for positive endeavour; they interpret its civilization and history; they represent its past struggle, and they plan for its future, as well as reflecting its projects and methods for confronting difficulties and challenges.

These programmes deal with general knowledge, philosophy, religion, the social sciences, language, the theoretical and applied sciences, the arts, literature, history, travel, biography, etc. It can safely be said that the Radio Service of the Hashemite Kingdom of Jordan is an extremely important school of culture, under the supervision of the Jordanian Ministry of Information which endeavours to make available the basic information required to raise the awareness of the people, widen their horizons and encourage their participation in matters of general concern.

### THE TELEVISION SERVICE

Jordan entered the television age with the start of official transmission on 27 April 1968. An official celebration was organized under the patronage of His Majesty King Hussein to mark the opening of the Jordan Television Service. Transmissions lasted four hours a day, and increased to five hours in October of the same year. Five years later, a second channel was introduced, so that thenceforth there were two channels: one broadcasting in Arabic and one in English, French and Hebrew.

By virtue of its charter, Jordanian Television is a government organization with a legal personality, administered by a Director-General under the authority of the Minister of Information. The head office of the organization is in Amman, and it is permitted to establish branches and offices in the kingdom, and to appoint representatives within Jordan and abroad. The organization has a special budget within the general state budget.

Jordanian Television is an organization concerned with education, information and entertainment. The charter states that this material shall be presented in a context acceptable to Jordanian and Arab tastes, in accordance with the general concepts of Jordanian national policy and its belief in unity of the two banks of the Jordan; as well as its belief in national aspirations for freedom, unity and improvement of life.

Television is the spearhead of the Jordanian information effort. It is always at the centre of transmission and reception of ideas. It is aware of its special responsibility for stimulating consciousness of new social and economic trends, and of the changes which the state development programmes are trying to bring about. It has responsibility for propounding values for the new society in the light of Jordans's development plans.

Because of its central role in the transmission and reception of ideas, the Television Service has established numerous departments. Of these, the programmes department is of a special interest to us. It is responsible for domestic production and for the selection of foreign programmes. In addition to entertainment, the Television Service broadcasts educational, religious and general and specialized cultural programmes.

An important part in the efforts of the Television Service to enlighten and instruct a wide circle of viewers, is played by the cultural and educational programmes broadcast in recent years on Channels 3 and 6. There are nine cultural programmes and light-educational programmes a week, representing respectively 18 and 16 per cent of all transmissions. For younger viewers, there are cartoons and locally produced children's programmes. The service also presents high-level cultural programmes, mainly dealing with matters of the Arab and Islamic heritage, contemporary Jordanian literature, the popular heritage and international literature. It has presented drama programmes dealing with the work of the Jordanian theatre and showing excerpts from some of its productions. From time to time, it has shown international plays in English on the mainly English-language Channel 6.

### THE PRESS

The appearance of the press in the area east of the Jordan was linked with the arrival of the Emir Abdullah. In 1920 in Ma'an, the Emir published a newspaper called *The Right Shall Triumph* with the slogan 'Revolutionary Arabism'. It was edited by Muhammad al-Ansi and Abd al-Latif Shakir. Four numbers were published in Ma'an and the fifth and last in Amman. In 1923, a newspaper called *The Arab Orient* was published, which was the official journal of the Government of Transjordan. In addition to proclamations, laws and decrees, it published literary and political articles and world news. The chief editor was Muhammad al-Shariqi.

In Palestine, the first newspaper to be published, in Jerusalem in 1908, was *The Ottoman Clarion*, owned by Ibrahim Zaka. In the same year, two other newspapers appeared: *Carmel* in Haifa, owned by Najib Nassar, and *Jerusalem* owned by George Hanania. In 1909, *The News* was published by Bandali Arabi, and also *Jewels* which was founded by Khalil Baidis. In 1911, *Palestine*, owned by Isa and Yusef al-Isa, came out and continued publication until 1967.

The history of the press derives from these two traditions. The number of political newspapers published to date is more than 100; and more than fifty periodicals of various types have also appeared. Press affairs in Jordan are regulated by a special law issued in 1955, Law No. 16 concerning Printed Material; this was amended in 1973. It gave the press the right to express opinions freely and to disseminate news by various means. On 16 March 1969, a Union of Journalists was formed; its members have valuable achievements to their credit in both the private and the public sphere. The union is affiliated to the Jordanian Professional Association, the National Association, the Federation of Arab Journalists and the International Press Association. It has concluded professional agreements with unions of journalists in many Arab countries, and has taken an active stand on many issues involving the press, especially those relating to the situation of Arab journalists in the occupied territories, whose case it has raised in all the Arab and international press congresses it has attended.

In view of the fact that 56.3 per cent of the entire population is concentrated in the province of Amman, it is not surprising that this province accounts for 70 per cent of newspaper circulation. Next comes the province of Irbid, with approximately 28.9 per cent of the population and 20 per cent of circulation. The remaining 10 per cent of circulation is accounted for by the provinces of Ma'an, Balqa and Karak.

The statistics published by the Economics Department of the Royal Scientific Society show that in 1976, 70.7 per cent of the population aged 12 years and above knew how to read and write as compared with 65.4 per cent in 1972. The distribution of the population between the ages of 12 and 65 by levels of education was as shown in Table 3.

The number of inhabitants of the East bank resident in the kingdom at the end of 1978 was 2,750,000.

Turning to the distribution as between provinces, we find that the

TABLE 3.           Population between ages 12 and 65
by level of education, 1976

| Educational level | percentage |
|---|---|
| Less than primary | 40.9 |
| Primary, but less than preparatory | 34.8 |
| Preparatory, but less than the complete secondary cycle | 12.5 |
| Completed secondary cycle | 7.8 |
| Post-secondary diploma | 1.5 |
| Completed university education (all levels) | 2.5 |
| | 100.0 |

province of Amman alone includes 66.5 per cent of all those possess general secondary education, and 77.49 per cent of those who have full university qualifications at all levels. Next comes the province of Irbid, where the corresponding percentages are 20.2 and 15.8. The province of Karak comes last with 2.8 and 1 per cent respectively.

Because it believes that newspapers and periodicals can play an effective role in the nation's cultural, social and economic and political advancement, the state has devoted special attention to the development of the press in the overall context of information and national development. The press has risen to the challenge and does all in its power to assist and facilitate the development of the country. It gives clear proof of its responsible attitude in a variety of ways: making known the state's point of view on the subjects under discussion; cementing national unity through the transmission of national culture; keeping readers informed of developments in science and technology, economics and the arts; promoting education and culture and strengthening the structure of political authority.

*Newspapers*

There are five Arabic-Language dailies: *al-Dustour* (the Constitution); *al-Rai* (Opinion), *al-Akhbar* (The News), *al-Sha'ab* (The People) and *al-Urdun* (Jordan); and one English-language daily, *The Jordan Times*, which has been published by the Jordanian Press Organization since 1975 and has a circulation of 8,000–10,000 copies. There are also various weeklies, including *al-Liwa* (The Flag), and *Akhbar al-Usbu'* (News of the Week). Of the Arabic language dailies, the oldest is *al-Dustour*, founded in 1967. It is published by the Jordanian Press and Publishing Company, and prints 25,000–35,000 copies per day. Then comes *al-Rai*, a political daily started in 1971 and published by the Jordanian Press Organization, which prints 42,000–50,000 copies per day. Next is *al-Akhbar*, a political daily started on 18 October 1975. This paper was suspended on 3 December 1975 and re-licensed on 21 December 1976. It prints 10,000–15,000 copies per day. *Al-Sha'ab* is a political daily published by the Popular Press, Printing and Publishing House. It was started at the beginning of 1976 and suspended on 15 September 1977. *Al-Urdun* is a political daily paper first published in Haifa in 1909. In 1923 it moved to Amman, and from 1927 onwards was published weekly. It continued as a weekly until the beginning of 1949, when it began to appear as a daily. It prints 4,000–6,000 copies.

The average number of copies of daily and weekly papers appearing each day in thus about 110,000, or 55 per 1,000 inhabitants. The number of copies per 1,000 inhabitants have developed over the years as follows: 1960—18; 1962—27; 1966—15; 1968—12; 1970—29; 1972—29; 1977—49; 1978—55. The statistics for 1972 were taken from the 1974 *Statistical Yearbook*. For 1977 and 1978, they are estimates by the owners of the newspapers. It is worth noting that the Jordanian daily and weekly press, in particular the Arabic-language portion, is distributed throughout the kingdom, as well as having distributors in most Arab countries where Jordanian citizens are living.

It can be seen from an examination of Jordanian newspapers, which normally consist of eight to twenty pages, that they rely principally on the news provided by the Jordanian News Agency, as well as by the principal international agencies and by other Arab and international newspapers. They provide day-to-day coverage of political events, as well as regular items on local news, sport, youth affairs, the occupied territories, cultural, scientific, educational and social issues, and the results of inquiries and surveys. They also have a readers' correspondence column and a local information page giving times of prayer, currency rates, duty doctors and chemists, television and radio programmes, etc. They have recently begun to devote two pages to photographic coverage of political and military events. There is also usually a 'Diary' column, as well as articles on Arab and international news, general-interest essays, obituaries and, finally, editorials, providing comment on current local, Arab and world events. Commercial advertisements take up about one-third of the space.

It will be obvious that the Jordanian press is a city, or more precisely an Amman, press, inasmuch as all the papers are published in the capital. They therefore cater mainly for an urban readership, and this inevitably tends to widen the cultural gap between the different segments of the population, notwithstanding the efforts made to provide comprehensive and responsible news coverage and other services to readers.

### The Ministry of Tourism and Antiquities

Early in 1967, a royal edict was issued placing both the Tourist Authority and the Public Department of Antiquities under the authority of a new ministry known as the Ministry of Tourism and Antiquities. This was the first time that responsibility for the two departments had been combined. The organization of the tourist sector had previously gone through a number of stages reflecting the lessons derived from Jordanian and foreign experience. In view of the growth of tourism and its obvious importance as a source of additional revenue, Law No. 70 establishing a Tourist Authority was promulgated at the start of 1960. The authority was given responsibility for developing the tourist potential of the country, with particular attention to the religious, archaeological and environmental aspects, and for drawing up and implementing programmes designed to attract tourists to Jordan and to make their stay enjoyable. In 1965, the government decided to review the authority's charter, and new legislation was issued under Provisional Law No. 45 of 1965 (subsequently promulgated as Law No. 10 of 1968). This law defined the objectives of the authority and made it responsible for encouraging and promoting tourism and for developing and exploiting the country's tourist potential so as to increase the national income and foster understanding among peoples.

The Ministry of Tourism and Antiquities aims to preserve and develop tourist sites; improve and take care of archaeological locations in co-operation with the Public Department of Antiquities; to supervise, control and develop tourist industries; provide facilities for the comfort and entertainment of tourists; facilitate procedures relating to tourists; devise and implement comprehensive publicity campaigns in co-operation with shops catering for tourists, of which there were about 218 in 1966, with 190 on the West bank, selling works of art and articles made from shells, olivewood and glass, as well as pottery, embroidery and traditional costumes.

The ministry, in co-operation with organizations such as Royal Jordanian Airlines (Alia), has prepared and marketed complete tourist programmes. It has also organized a number of joint tourist information and poster campaigns. In co-operation with certain magazines, it has prepared special numbers on Jordan as seen from the tourist's point of view, for example, the special number published by the magazine *Journal de Voyages*, and the guide published by the Ottoman Bank in Amman.

A special supplement published recently by the *Financial Times*, said that Jordan has had conspicuous success in the field of tourism during the past three years and that the Jordanian Government has taken the initiative in co-ordinating infrastructural development. There is a monthly bulletin, *Jordanian Tourism*, published by the Directorate of Tourist Information in the ministry, and an English-language publication regularly issued by the ministry since 1974 under the title, *Jordan: Special Tourism Issue*. An association of dealers in oriental works of art has been formed, to promote the manufacture of articles for sale to tourists and the participation of Jordanian dealers in international trade fairs. It is also worth noting that meetings of the Tourist Authority are presided over by His Highness Prince Muhammad.

The Five-year Development Plan required the Ministry of Tourism and Antiquities to amend the legislation on tourism; to continue co-operation with Royal Jordanian Airlines (Alia) and the Association of Jordanian Tourist and Travel Offices in carrying out marketing programmes; to increase the ministry's allocations for the production of tourist publications and posters; to hold training courses for tourist guides; to organize an international festival in Aqaba, an annual artistic festival, with the accent on entertainment, in Jarash, and regular festivals in Azraq and by the Dead Sea; to continue to encourage the private sector to invest in tourism, and to support, develop and stimulate traditional and souvenir industries.

### ANTIQUITIES

On 17 July 1923, it was decided to establish a scientific academy in the region east of the Jordan. In a letter to the President of the Commissioners, the Head of the Emir's Secretariat stated: 'Wishing to encourage the study of our ancient monuments and to raise aloft the torch of Arab learning, His Highness has issued a decree to establish a scientific academy.' The members were given the task of supervising archaeological activities. At the beginning of September 1923, a law was promulgated establishing a Department of Archaeology to 'protect the country's monuments from destruction, and to collect together, in the region and under the control of the people, the things which have been dispersed'. It was decided to place this department under the authority of the President of the Commissioners.

In 1925, maintenance work began in Jarash and the crusader castle at Karak. In the next year, maintenance work was extended to the castle of Rabd in Ajlun. In the same year, the first bulletin was published on archaeology in the region east of the Jordan.

In 1936, Lancaster Harding took over the post of Inspector of Antiquities for the region east of the Jordan. In 1948, he was given responsibility for a wide area of Palestine, the region in which the Dead Sea scrolls were discovered. Harding was able to visit, record and photograph most of the archaeological sites east of the Jordan. Then, in 1951, the Jordanian Archaeological Museum was set up in the citadel, to include exhibits going back to the Stone Age and continuing up to the Islamic period. The first number of the *Annual of the Jordanian Department of Antiquities* was published. The Department of Antiquities was made part of the Department of Education. Since 1956, there has been a succession of Jordanian directors of the department, who have implemented the general policy established for it. A number of laws regarding the antiquities of the region east of the Jordan have been promulgated, including Law No. 133 of 1953 which specified that an antiquity is 'any fixed or transportable object, created, formed, carved, painted or built by man, or discovered, produced or adapted by him, before A.D. 1700'. This law defined the condition that must be met by any expedition before it can be licensed to excavate or search in archaeological sites. The general policy of the department has been clearly laid down since 1967, when a royal edict appointing a Minister for Tourism and Antiquities was published. Article 3 of Provisional Law No. 13 of 1976 concerning Antiquities, which came into effect on 16 February 1976, stated that the department was to be entrusted with the tasks and responsibilities connected with the implementation of the state's archaeological policy, and with evaluating the antiquity of objects and sites and estimating the importance of all archaeological remains. The department has accordingly assumed responsibility for the administration, supervision, protection, maintenance and recording of antiquities throughout the kingdom, with the preservation and recording of these antiquities, and for the improvement of their surroundings; for exhibiting antiquities and disseminating knowledge of archaeology; for establishing archaeological centres and museums; for searching for remains throughout the kingdom, and helping with organization of museums belonging to the government, including historical, artistic and folklore museums; for co-operating with local, Arab and foreign agencies in serving the heritage and promoting archaeological awareness in accordance with the relevant laws and statutes. It is also responsible for ensuring that antiquities are acquired and disposed of in accordance with the provisions of the Law on Antiquities, and of the relevant statutes, decisions and directives.

### Museums

*The Palestine Archaeological Museum in Jerusalem.* The foundation stone of this museum was laid by the British High Commissioner, Sir John Chancellor, on 19 June 1930. On 13 January 1938, the museum was opened to visitors. The museum included a 35,000-volume library containing valuable source material on the archaeology, art, history, religion and geography of Palestine and the neighbouring region. The ownership of the museum was transferred to the Jordanian Government after the end of the British mandate in Palestine. In the June 1967 war, the Israeli army entered the museum and took over its treasures, while Jewish archaeologists transferred the Dead Sea scrolls to the Israeli museum on the other side of Jerusalem.

*The Jordanian Museum of Archaeology.* This museum was established on the top of the Jabal al-Qal'a (the Hill of the Citadel) in 1951, and all the neighbouring sites were considered as attached to it. When the Jordanian Department of Archaeology took over this building, it transferred its offices there. It also transferred to this building the Jordanian archaeological items which had been exhibited in the Palestine Museum in Jerusalem until 1947, when they had been returned to Amman and kept in store until the new museum was built.

### Excavations

Since its creation, the Department of Antiquities has undertaken a wide range of activities in many different parts of the country. It has succeeded in discovering many archaeological sites and items. The most important excavations and search projects undertaken by or through the department or under its auspices have included the excavations of Qumran and the Dead Sea scrolls; Ain al-Fushkha; Ai; the Tulaylat al-Ghassul; Tell al-Fari'a; Samira; Jerusalem; the Temple; the excavations at Petra and Amman; the discoveries at Fahl; al-Quwaylaba; Deir'Alla; Tell al-Sa'idia; Takim; Dutan; Azraq; al-Jeib; Dhiban; al-Fardis; Khirbet al-Tanur; Tell al-Khalifa; Rum; al-Beida; Ariha; Qasr Burqu; al-Mukhit; Siyagha; Qasr al-Bint at Petra; Dhat al-Ras; Tabqa Fahl; etc.

Of the many organizations involved in Jordanian archaeology over the years, the majority have tended to be British, French, German or American. While excavations in the area as a whole began over a century ago, the part of it east of the river Jordan received only marginal attention, principally expressed in the form of travellers' observations and of surface surveys.

The number of archaeological sites on the East bank is estimated to be more than 500. As for Palestine, there were estimated to be more than 2,862 sites in the region in 1944. On the East bank, from 1952 to the present day, excavations have been carried out involving more than 100 sites, compared with hundreds of sites in Palestine. Each number of the *Annual of the Jordanian Department of Antiquities* now contains a description of the excavations carried out during the previous year, especially those whose results represent a real advance in knowledge.

The first excavations in the area east of the Jordan were those carried out on part of the Jabal al-Qal'a in Amman by an Italian expedition during the years 1927, 1929, 1930, 1937 and 1939. These excavations (of which only preliminary reports were published) cleared part of a Roman temple and part of a Byzantine/Islamic building to the north of it.

When it was decided to build the Amman museum on the Jabal al-Qal'a, Harding immediately carried out excavations on the site. In the same year (1949), a group of Ammonite statues was discovered on the north-west part of the hill, outside the Roman walls. During the period 1929–38, the Pontifical Biblical Institute undertook excavations in the Tulaylat al-Ghassul, and found astonishing remains dating back to the Chalcolithic period. For a number of years, starting in 1933, the Franciscan Biblical Institute carried out excavations in Khirbet al-Mukhit and in Siyagha, which some consider to be Nebo, where the prophet Moses died.

The principal discoveries during these excavations were some Byzantine churches. In 1937, Nelson Glueck discovered an imposing Nabataean temple in Khirbet al-Tanur. Also, small exploratory trenches were dug at Adr and Khirbet bil-Wa'. A number of graves were discovered dating back to the late Bronze Age or Iron Age in Amman, Saheb, Amqablin and Madaba. Between 1951 and 1953, the American School of Oriental Studies in Jerusalem undertook major excavations in Dhiban, the capital of the Moabites, but the results were not published until 1964 and 1972. This was quite apart from, the excavations carried out by the University of Jordan between 1973 and 1977, which led to extremely important discoveries, especially in the area of Tell al-Mazar.

Since the beginning of the nineteenth century, a considerable number of travellers and pilgrims have visited our region, including the famous Burckhardt. Plans were made for a survey of the East bank to be carried out in 1970, when an agreement was reached between the Association of the Palestine Exploration Fund and the recently created American Association for the Exploration of Palestine, under which the first organization would survey and map Palestine, while the American Association would do the same work east of the Jordan. The Association of the Fund achieved its objective, but the American Association failed to carry out its project in the area east of the Jordan. In 1881, the Association of the Fund decided to undertake the east-bank survey itself, one volume of its findings being published in London in 1883. It was not until 1949 that an accurate map of the east-bank area was produced, by the Department of Lands and Survey in Amman.

After the discovery of the importance of pottery in archaeological dating, a number of archaeologists carried out surface explorations of the east-bank area, collecting pottery that could shed some light on the history of the various sites. They did similar work in the area east of the Dead Sea, in the Jordan basin and in the area of al-Salt. The most important archaeological survey of the east bank was carried out by Nelson Glueck between 1930 and 1949. Glueck published his preliminary findings in a large number of articles dealing with his discoveries in the area south of Dhiban, south of Jal'ad and Ammun, and north of the river of Zarqa as far as Huran, etc.

Archaeology in Jordan is a many-sided subject, which has developed enormously over the years. Archaeological surveys have confirmed that there are treasures in Jordan still buried underground. It is certain that their discovery will produce new ideas which will change many of the theories of historians and archaeologists.

### The future plans of the Department
### of Antiquities in the light of development plans

The Jordanian Department of Antiquities has taken on the task of forming a Higher Council for Archaeology, made up of a number of specialists and prominent personalities in the field of archaeology, to be responsible for formulating archaeological policy and arranging the necessary finance. It is also in touch with relevant organizations both at home and abroad, and has concluded bilateral agreements with Arab and foreign countries to strengthen co-operation in the field of archaeology. The department has collaborated with the University of Jordan in excavations and surveys. There has also been co-operation with foreign organizations and schools in joint excavations and in the conservation of finds. The department has in addition called in experts from friendly bodies, organizations and universities to advise on the technical aspects of archaeological operations. Special priority has been given to expanding the Jordanian Museum of Archaeology in Amman so that it can be a centre for scientific and cultural activity and tourism, and to establishing branch museums in other cities. There are also plans to introduce travelling exhibitions.

The department is currently meeting the needs of certain Arab states by providing them with expertise and information in the framework of the Arab League and of ALECSO. It is also engaged in preparing a bilingual

(Arabic and English) index of all archaeological sites on both the east and west banks of the River Jordan.

The department occasionally presents exhibitions of Jordanian antiquities outside the country. The most important of these was the exhibition on the Nabataeans in Lyons, France. The department is also carrying out joint excavations with the Syrian Department of Archaeology and Museums in the city of Bosra al-Sham, which was one of the ten cities (Decapolis) in the Roman period, so as to uncover the Nabataean remains in the city.

### The Ministry of Wakfs (religious endowments), Islamic Affairs and Shrines

This ministry was created in 1967. It had previously been called the Department of Wakfs and Islamic Affairs. The Ministry was able to make important progress and to develop its capacity and administrative apparatus, following the publication of its Law No. 32 of 1970, amending Law No. 26 of 1966, concerning Wakfs, Islamic Affairs and Shrines, which defined the objectives of the ministry as: (a) the preservation of mosques and endowed properties; (b) attention to general matters and social problems; (c) the promotion of the Mosque, to enable it to carry out its mission in society in the fields of Islamic education and co-ordination between the organizations offering guidance, whether in the educational, social or information fields; (d) the establishment of links between the mosque and these organizations, so as to promote the progress and prosperity of Jordanian society; (e) the stimulation of a spirit of sacrifice and the strengthening of spiritual values; (f) the development and consolidation of Islamic morality and its establishment in the lives of Muslims; (g) the fostering of general Islamic activity and religious education; (h) the creation of religious centres and Koranic schools; (i) the dissemination of Islamic culture and the preservation of the Islamic heritage; (j) the highlighting of the role of Islamic civilization in human progress; (k) the development of religious awareness; and (l) the consolidation of intellectual and religious relationships and links.

The ministry has greatly increased the number of preachers and spiritual instructors responsible for instructing and admonishing Muslims and strengthening them in the Islamic creed. It publishes a monthly magazine, The Way of Islam, which appears on the first day of each Hijra month. Each issue of this magazine contains articles dealing with a given aspect of life. The ministry also issues religious, educational and cultural studies from time to time, and has printed and published a number of religious books. In the field of education, the ministry used to finance the college of Islamic Law which was incorporated in the University of Jordan in 1971, and it continues to administer a number of religious schools and courts of Islamic Law.

The Five-year Development Plan specified that the ministry be concerned with the spiritual condition, beliefs and Islamic and moral values of the Jordanian people, together with their capacities, skills and achievements. This concern is expressed in the building of mosques; in the provision of qualified Imams (prayer-leaders) to give guidance, to improve morals and to strengthen faith; in the building of schools, libraries and social and humanitarian organizations which can act as intellectual beacons and play a genuinely effective role in developing spiritual and intellectual qualities, and in guiding conduct; in concern with historical and political documents and Islamic manuscripts; in spreading Islamic culture throughout society; in supporting the libraries of mosques and creating a general library in the Ministry of Endowments.

The ministry is now preparing plans for the construction of the King Abdullah Mosque in Amman, and for setting up rest-houses for travellers at the two Abu Ubeida shrines in al-Ghur and al-Mazar in Karak.

This sector is distinguished from other sectors by the fact that part of its costs are voluntarily borne by a very large number of citizens who have donated part or all of their property and estates for works of charity. The ministry controls these *wakfs*, or endowments, which are perpetual and constantly increasing, and plans to set up cultural centres as new donations are made in Irbid, Zarqa and Amman, which will primarily be concerned with instruction in the Holy Koran.

### Children's cultural centres

Cultural centres have been established in many parts of the kingdom, with the aim of helping children to develop and giving them purposeful cultural instruction, so that they will be better equipped to use their free time in creative activity of an artistic or cultural nature. The centres also aim to encourage children to read and draw, to play games that will develop their abilities, to take part in competitions and to solve puzzles and problems.

It is part of the policy of these centres to establish more children's libraries and extend library services to villages and remote rural areas in order to promote the attainment of cultural, informative and social objectives. In this way, the library will become complementary to general educational planning. The policy also involves organizing exhibitions and taking them to remote areas, explaining essential concepts by pictures and other methods and encouraging children to take an interest in the theatre and the cinema, listen to live and recorded music, radio programmes, etc., and watch selected television programmes, especially cartoons.

Children's books have been produced since the early 1950s, at first as a result of individual initiative and more recently under the auspices of the Royal Scientific Society, which established a specialist committee for the purpose. There are also two children's magazines: *Paris*, first published in 1971, and *Samir*, first published in 1977. In addition, the magazine *Arts* has

he marble head of Tyche, the Goddess
rtune (Roman period), found in the
ian Citadel.

asr el-Karana. The only Omayyad
e built as a fortress, it was built in the
h century A.D. and was used primarily
hunting lodge and for relaxation.

os: Jordanian National
mission for Unesco.

1

3

4

3. On the floor of the Greek Orthodox church in the little town of Madaba is the famous sixth-century mosaic map of Palestine. It depicts the towns of Palestine and shows monasteries and churches down to the northern Nile. In the centre is a plan of the city of Jerusalem with its walls, churches, houses and streets.

4. Centuries of rubble and sand had half covered this noble Roman Forum in Jerash, whose modern town can be seen in the distance. This was the hub and civic centre of the Roman provincial town, one of the free Decapolis cities of the first centuries B.C. and A.D. The Forum with its Ionic columns dates from the earlier building period in Jerash.

5. The Monastery (Ed-Deir), Petra. This gigantic building carved into a mountain-top cliff is believed to have been a Nabataean temple, but at some time was used as a Christian church as indicated by crosses carved into its walls. It probably dates from the third century B.C.

6. The Roman theatre is Amman's most impressive monument and dates back to the second and third centuries A.D. It has a seating capacity of 6,000. In the background is a general view of Amman.

5

6

7. Amman, al-Hussein Sport City,
The Pavilion.

8. The main gate of the University
of Jordan.

7

8

devoted considerable space to cultural and other questions affecting children.

On the principle that the creation of a new type of man starts with the child, a number of cultural centres have been established to promote the sound development of children. These centres include: the Princess Hayya Cultural Centre; the Club of Friends of the Child; the Association of Friends of the Child; the Children's Cultural Section in the Department of Culture and Arts; the Children's Section in the Jordanian Television Service; and the Children's Centre in the Federation of Charitable Associations.

Each of these centres performs its tasks well. But perhaps the biggest and most important of them is the Princess Hayya Cultural Centre, founded in 1976, which represents a new departure in this field.

## THE PRINCESS HAYYA CULTURAL CENTRE

This centre aims to help children to use their free time for artistic and cultural activity. It also aims to implant the habits of reading, drawing, discussion and enjoyment of the fine arts and to give children sufficient preparation to enable them to absorb their national culture and history. To be more precise, the aim of the centre is to create a generation of young people with a wide range of perception, an understanding of their surroundings, and a balanced approach to everyday life, so that they can form a valuable nucleus for their society, for Arab society and for the world in general.

Economic and social development can occur only if children receive a sound upbringing that equips them to bring about changes in a spirit of responsibility and awareness. The future of Jordan will undoubtedly depend on the care taken to ensure the sound development of the nation's children, and it is to the achievement of this aim that the centre is dedicated. Initially established in the capital, Amman, it rapidly extended its activities to other towns in which it opened subcentres, so that its impact has been nation-wide.

The Princess Hayya Cultural Centre, which was established on 14 November 1976, is a charitable organization run by a council of trustees made up of private citizens and officials well known for their interest in social and cultural work. Her Highness Princess Basma is the President. The centre helps the home and the school to develop social and cultural awareness in children during their free time, by engaging them in co-operative and socially oriented activity.

The statutes of the centre stipulate that every child aged from 6 to 16 has the right to join the centre, and to benefit from its services and its library. As most of its members are at school, the services of the centre are brought to their classrooms, under the supervision of their teachers. The centre intends to create about fifty subcentres, each with a library of 10,000 books, together with a theatre, cinema and arts-room. From time to time, the centre undertakes visits to children in remote areas, in the desert, in camps and in villages. It distributes books to these children from its 1,500-volume travelling library.

*Principal activities of the centre*

*The library.* The Amman centre has a library of 7,000 books, mostly in Arabic. There are some books in English and in other languages. The centre has taken its concern with language to the point of starting a section to print and publish children's books, with special emphasis on quality in both appearance and content, and with the Arab heritage, history and traditions as the main source of inspiration. The centre has published its first book for children, and has co-operated with the Iranian Centre for the Development of Children in translating four Iranian books into Arabic and publishing them.

*The theatre.* The centre considers the theatre to be a highly effective medium for developing the character of children and widening their perceptions. Teachers and actors instruct children in this sphere, and teach them the importance of correct speech and the art of listening. A drama group started by the centre gave its first performances in the centre's theatre, which sent 300 people, and is planning to tour schools and branch centres in the provinces.

*The Fine Arts, Manual Crafts and Hobbies.* The centre has the necessary training equipment to help children develop their talents in drawing, designing, carving, pottery, music, first-aid, cinematography and scouting.

*Photography.* As children are affected by their exposure to television and the cinema, the centre stresses the importance of helping them to become the masters of this medium rather than its servants. It accordingly gives them an opportunity to learn the art of cinematography, and all aspects of photography are explained to them, including lighting, sound and preparation of scripts. There are plans to establish a tele-vision-production group.

The centre's current projects can be summarized as: establishing a training complex for children; starting a museum to tell children about Jordanian and Arab civilization and the civilizations of other countries; setting up an open-air theatre-in-the-round with seating for about 800 people, to be used for musical and other cultural events presented by Jordanian and visiting groups; constructing an aviary, an indoor sports arena and another hall to be used as a gymnasium.

On the occasion of the International Year of the Child, the centre announced a monthly competition for books designed for children, whether fiction, drama, short stories or poetry. It offered prizes in recognition of achievement by children in the fields of musical performance (instrumental or vocal), mimicry, poetry or short-story reading. It also held exhibitions of children's books and drawings. It presented plays and started a factory for producing children's games, as well as publishing a number of books.

# Aspects of cultural activity

## Characteristics of the literary movement

Literary activity in Jordan has developed in every direction, starting with poetry, going on to drama and ending with stories, works of fiction and academic studies. As regards form, content and general character, all this literature has a close and easily discernible relationship with that of the Arab world as a whole. Jordan has made a major contribution to the progress of modern Arab literature, in terms of both quantity and quality. It has played a central role in Arab political life ever since the First World War—when its modern history began—and has managed at the same time to form and establish itself as a state and to maintain its fundamental strategic position throughout the turmoils and vicissitudes of more than half a century.

The upheaval of 1948 brought unity to the two banks of the Jordan, and the new entity thus created proceeded to make its mark throughout the Arab and non-Arab world. Jordan has helped to provide the Arab world with an enormous number of workers and trained personnel. It has made a similar contribution in the intellectual and cultural sphere: Jordanian writers and scholars from both the East and the West banks are to be found all over the world, especially in the major centres of intellectual dissemination and related activity.

### FORMS OF INTELLECTUAL AND LITERARY ACTIVITY

#### Translation

Jordanian and Palestinian translators have, in the first instance, concerned themselves with Russian and French literature. They have given the European heritage to the Arab literary world. They have concentrated particularly on translating works of philosophy, literature and law. Some of them have translated works on modern politics.

## Study of the heritage

Jordanians and Palestinians have played a major role in the study of the heritage. Any mention of the principal researchers in the Arab world must include the names of Jordanian researchers, whose methods are among the most advanced. We must also mention the Jordanian Academy of the Arabic Language, which has been concerned with analysing and disseminating the heritage since its foundation.

## Literary criticism

It is clear from the volume of critical studies published, that Jordanian academics are in advance of their non-Jordanian counterparts in this field. The scarcity of good criticism produced by non-academics is probably a natural phenomenon, since modern criticism needs a high level of culture and precise methods of work.

## Poetry

Here mention must first be made of the traditionalists, a group of highly esteemed poets who are perhaps the leading figures of the modern romantic school in the Arab world. Next come the young poets who have been influenced by the modern school. This school aims at a poetic vision in which the perception and expression of truth and beauty are grounded in an authentic experience of reality, the land is an abiding source of inspiration and the great issues confronting mankind are not shirked.

The fact that there is an active poetry movement has, of course, led to different poetic tendencies on the technical level. The first tendency is found among the poets who have kept to the traditional poetic forms, especially the customary Arab use of rhyme. These poets strive for an impressive effect, and seek their inspiration in the heritage. The second tendency partakes of both the old and the new, in that it started traditionally and subsequently developed. The third tendency is contemporary and modern, and aims at presenting new visions of reality and of the world. These poets have moved away from 'occasional' poetry, and have offered new intellectual and aesthetic values. Some collections of poems published on both the East and West banks express this tendency strongly. It is also true that collections by the poets who appeared in the occupied territory during the 1960s and the 1970s have taken the Arab world by storm, and occupy an important place in the minds and hearts of Arab youth. A number of Arabists have also translated some of the collections that have appeared into other languages.

### Fiction

The art of fiction was introduced into Palestine and Jordan at the turn of the century, initially through translations. Eventually a new generation of fiction writers appeared, who were in direct contact with Arab literature, and who borrowed its artistic methods, its rules and concepts. This new generation came into its own in the early 1960s, with the development of new forms for both realist and romantic fiction. Even where the content remained traditional, the voices that spoke through it were fresh and exciting. In fact, the shared reality that linked the life of the people of Jordan with the people of Palestine after the catastrophe made this disaster and its consequences into a common denominator between writers of both banks, all of whom have drawn their inspiration from the tragedy and day-to-day problems of the refugees. Social and environmental issues are also not neglected, so it can be said that Jordanian fiction is realist fiction, even when it appears in an imaginative garb. As with poetry, some novels and short stories have been translated into other languages.

### Drama

Since the creation of the modern Jordanian state, the theatrical movement has progressed through a number of phases, marked by the activities of the teaching theatre, the university theatre group, the Jordanian theatre group, the private-sector theatre and, most recently, the theatre of the Department of Culture and Arts, which is administered by a board known as the Committee for the Drama Sector and composed of leading figures in the theatrical world.

### Cultural Associations

Numerous cultural associations have been formed since the establishment of the modern Jordanian state. Their activities have been centred in the principal towns of Jordan. These associations typify, in their activities, the various stages of the revolutionary struggle against foreign occupation and against the Mandate, quite apart from their concern for cultural matters. In the period of the emirate and the start of the monarchy in the region east of the Jordan, associations of this type had already sprung up in response to cultural needs and were laying firm foundations for their future work. They deserve honourable mention as one of the numerous phenomena which graced the cultural movement. Perhaps the most distinguished and important of them was the Association of the Emir Abdullah, who founded the Jordanian State in 1921. The Emir was a writer and poet, and his court contained a group of outstanding Syrian, Iraqi and Lebanese poets and writers, who were treated with conspicuous generosity.

61

The Emir's Association is bound to figure prominently in any history of the cultural movement in Jordan. Its numerous congresses, devoted to literary and intellectual questions, were largely responsible for the nation's cultural awakening. There was scarcely a writer in the region east of the Jordan during the Emir's reign who did not participate in these congresses and benefit from the Emir's personal attention and care. In addition, poets and men of letters from all over the Arab world flocked to the palace, where the Emir welcomed them warmly and engaged them in literary discussions, setting aside completely the cares of politics and government. His association thus became a cultural club, the records of whose debates and discussions were eagerly studied in literary gatherings in Jordan and abroad. The Emir's Association played a central role in literary life during more than a quarter of a century. It was also an academy for literature and science, from which other associations branched off and spread rapidly to the major cities. These associations and groups, which brought together many different activities, included: the Arab Catholic Youth League in Madaba (1922); the Okaz Club in Ajlum (1929); the Homentmen Club, which was founded in Amman in 1936 and renamed the Youth Sports Club in 1946; the Jordan Club (1941); the Ahli Club (1944); the Youth Sports and Cultural Club (1946); the Al-Jazira Club (1947); and the New Generation Club, founded in 1950. These clubs endeavoured to promote both sports and culture. In the cultural sphere, their activities included the organization of lectures, plays, concerts and debates. Some of them, for example the Youth Sports and Cultural Club and the Homentmen Club, also ran libraries and wall magazines and issued publications.

Clubs in both the provinces and the capital participated in cultural activity, during this period, the main centres being al-Salt and Irbid. The Arab Club founded in Irbid in 1945 had a library, and its administrative committee organized seminars, lectures, tours and discussion groups. It also concerned itself with the cultural aspects of broadcasting, encouraged amateur activities and endeavoured to stimulate progress generally. The same was true of the Caucasian Club in Zarqa, founded in 1945, and of the various cultural groups established in al-Salt in the early 1940s.

In the 1950s and 1960s, the scope of these associations widened in Amman and in the other provinces. Clubs were founded in every town. In al-Salt, the al-Salt Club was founded in 1952. In 1964, the Olympic Club and the al-Jazira Club were founded in Amman. The Youth Club in Amman, later known as the Sporting and Cultural Renaissance Club, was founded in 1965, as were the Youth Club, the al-Salt Sporting Club, and the Karak Cultural Club. At about this time, similar clubs were founded in the remaining cities of Jordan. All these clubs were linked to the Youth Welfare Organization when it was created. This organization is the body responsible for promoting the welfare and advancement of young people and encouraging their physical and cultural development, a concern that recently found practical expression when the organization began to collaborate with the Department of Culture and Arts in Amman in providing the provinces with the cultural facilities to which they are entitled. It was within the framework of this collaboration that the Department of Culture and Arts presented dramatic performances and travelling exhibitions of books, the graphic arts, etc. The clubs referred to above combined concern with sports and concern with culture. The same is true of the various charitable associations established at all levels of the community. Among the associations that have taken part in cultural work are: the al-Salt Charitable Association; the Association of Northeners; the Islamic Science League; the 'White League' family associations; the Association of Christian Girls; the Association of Muslim Girls; the Club of Graduates of the Arab University of Beirut; the Club of Graduates of the American University; the Circassian Charitable Association, etc.

There are also literary clubs whose activities have lain wholly in the cultural fields. These clubs, which appeared in the 1930s and 1940s and in the early 1950s, were founded in accordance with the aims of the Emir's Association, and have done much to stimulate interest not only in literature but in culture generally. They still represent a link with the intellectual influences created by the great Arab revolt. Clubs of this type in Amman are: the Literary Association; the Library Club; the Club for Cultural Co-operation; the King Hussein Club; the Arab Association, the Generation Club; the Intellectual League. Through their effective participation in constructive intellectual and cultural work, they have made an important contribution to contemporary Jordanian culture and to Arab culture as a whole.

The existence of the League of Jordanian writers, founded in 1974, was certainly a result of the work started by the founders of these associations. The aims of the league were in complete harmony with the aims of the associations and clubs which had appeared since the creation of the Jordanian state.

This league was created from a constituent council made up of fifteen writers. Its aims are to open up channels of communication between the culture of Jordan and that of the Arab and non-Arab world as a whole. It also aims to strengthen links between Jordanian writers and literary and cultural organizations everywhere. It is directed by an administrative council, assisted by committees for fiction, poetry, drama, the cinema, studies and other matters. The league is supported materially and in other ways by the Ministry of Culture and Youth. It serves the development of culture in Jordan through its publication programmes and by organizing lectures, seminars, study groups, literary festivals, artistic exhibitions and similar events. The league is a full member of the Permanent Bureau of the Federation of Arab Writers, and of the Federation of Afro-Asian Writers.

The cultural associations have thus contributed a great deal to the development and advancement of culture in Jordan, and the work of the original founders of these associations will continue to be a solid support for the nation's overall cultural edifice.

## Libraries and documentation centres

Libraries and documentation centres are considered to be a basic element of culture. They are the cultural barometer of the country, in that they provide a reliable indication of the cultural level of achievement of a particular region in all spheres of knowledge. Jordan soon became aware of this, and gave special attention and priority to libraries, to the point of becoming a pioneer in libraries and documentation in the Middle East. It was able to do so because of the solid scientific and technical foundations on which its development was based. The following is a brief description of the Jordanian library system and its development.

*Library centres*, such as the libraries section established in 1958 in the Ministry of Education and Instruction. This is the section responsible for the ministry's libraries, such as school libraries, libraries of institutes and technical schools, libraries belonging to the administration, and mobile libraries. The section has also participated directly or indirectly in the development of other libraries in Jordan. Another example of these centres is the Association of Jordanian Libraries, created at the end of 1963. This association has co-ordinated and unified library activities in Jordan. Since its creation it has supervised the training of some 700 librarians, and in 1976 its efforts in this field were crowned by the establishment of a Centre for Library and Information Science. It publishes a magazine, *Library Bulletin*, founded in 1965, and has also published a number of books. This association is the link between libraries in Jordan, the Arab countries and the rest of the world. Since 1967, it has been a member of the International Federation of Library Associations and Institutions.

The Directorate of Libraries in the Ministry of Culture and Youth was founded in 1977. This Directorate will undoubtedly play an effective role in supporting the development of libraries, especially public libraries and a national library, which Jordan still does not possess; this was noted in the directorate's statutes, issued in 1977.

*Libraries* (academic libraries; school libraries; children's libraries; public libraries; specialist and government libraries). All these libraries have played a fundamental role in supporting and advancing the library movement in Jordan. Examples of academic libraries are the library of the University of Jordan, founded at the end of 1962, and the Library of the University of Yarmouk, founded in 1976. As regards libraries attached to institutes, there are seven libraries belonging to the Ministry of Education and Instruction, one library supervised by the United Nations Relief and Work Agency (UNRWA), and two libraries attached to institutes in the private sector. There are academic libraries attached to government organizations specializing in different fields, such as the Library of the College of Nursing in the al-Hussein Medical Complex; the Library of the Social

Institute; and the Library of the Institute of Islamic Law Studies. School libraries and children's libraries are considered to be important for the development of reading and learning skills. The Ministry of Education and Instruction has been concerned with school libraries since 1958, when it ordered a separate room to be set aside as a library in secondary schools. It has also started mobile libraries which cover all provinces and districts. There are now thirteen of them, offering their services to all government schools in Jordan. UNRWA has recently started to establish similar libraries in some parts of Amman.

It is worth noting that there are two categories of children's libraries in Jordan: those attached to public libraries and those run by children's associations. The Association of Friends of the Child has started two libraries in Amman, and the Princess Hayya Cultural Centre, established in 1976, offers library, cultural and artistic services to children.

The public libraries, which offer their services to everyone without exception, are controlled by the municipalities. The first public library to be established in Jordan was that of Irbid, in 1957. It was followed by those in Amman (1960), Karak (1962), Ma'an (1964), Zarqa and al-Salt (1965), etc. Finally, there are the specialist and government libraries, covering specific subjects and catering for specialized readerships. At the head of these libraries in Jordan is the Library of the Royal Scientific Society, founded in 1970. Then comes the Library of the Central Bank (1964), specializing in economics and banking; the Library of the Department of Meteorology (1965); the Library of the Natural Resources Authority (1966); the Library of the Hospital of the University of Jordan; the Library of the Association of Lawyers; the Library of the Union of Engineers; the Library of the Radio Service, etc. Libraries in this category are not necessarily confined to printed matter: there are, for example the film libraries of the Radio Service (1958) and of the Ministry of Education and Instruction (1960); and the Library of the Television Organization (1970).

*Documentation centres.* The duties of these centres, which specialize in specific subjects, include the provision of information services to specialists. Various methods are used for this purpose, including bulletins, summaries, indexes and abstracts and other rapid-information and source-transfer techniques.

The first centre of this kind to be established in Jordan was the Educational Documentation Section set up by the Ministry of Education and Instruction in 1964. The University of Jordan established a documents and records section, attached to the history section of the faculty of Literature, in 1974, and the Ministry of Agriculture established an agricultural documentation section in 1976.

Jordan intends to expand its network of libraries and need of documentation and information centres still further. In this context it will issue such additional legislation as may be necessary concerning libraries, especially public libraries, and will implement plans for the establishment of a National Library, which will play an important part in effecting co-ordination and co-operation between all libraries in Jordan, and between them and their counterparts abroad. The Ministry of Culture and Youth will play a major role in developing and supporting libraries in Jordan, and in helping to ensure that the nation enjoys a library service fully up to international standards in every sphere of its activities.

## Writing, translation and publication

As far as writing, translation and publication are concerned, Jordan is an inseparable part of the Arab world. Nevertheless, the situation in Jordan is somewhat different from that obtaining in neighbouring Arab countries, in that these activities are more closely linked with numerous factors, such as the encouragement given to research and the carrying out of studies dealing with various subjects in different areas of knowledge. This has resulted in a conspicuous role being played by academic and similar institutions such as universities, mosques, cultural associations and centres, etc.

The public sector has supported literary activity by publishing and marketing printed material, especially after the character of the reading public, whose interaction with the writer is a necessary fact of cultural life, was formed, after libraries and information centres were set up and institutions relating to the different aspects of the book world established (such as library associations, authors' leagues and federations of writers and publishers). Information about literary activities in Jordan is now made available on a regular basis at local, regional and international levels.

Writing, translation and publishing in any country have a cultural and

TABLE 4.  Output of original works and translations, 1967–78

| Year | Original works | Translations | Total |
|------|---------------|--------------|-------|
| 1967 | 26 | 7 | 33 |
| 1968 | 39 | 3 | 42 |
| 1969 | 60 | 5 | 65 |
| 1970 | 50 | 3 | 53 |
| 1971 | 57 | 3 | 60 |
| 1972 | 78 | 2 | 80 |
| 1973 | 93 | 3 | 96 |
| 1974 | 82 | 3 | 85 |
| 1975 | 88 | 2 | 90 |
| 1976 | 65 | 3 | 68 |
| 1977 | 107 | 5 | 112 |
| 1978 | 189 | 7 | 196 |
| | 934 | 46 | 980 |

intellectual significance, and reflect the concern of the country in question for its culture. Leaving aside textbooks, government publications, newspapers and periodicals, we obtain the following statistics for these activities in Jordan.

Concerning original writing, translation and reports, the number of books to appear during the period 1967–78 was 980; an average of 81.66 books per year. 92 per cent of these were original works, 5 per cent were translations and 3 per cent were reports. Of these books, 97 per cent were published in Arabic, 1.7 per cent in English, 0.5 per cent in Italian, 0.3 per cent in French, 0.2 per cent in Spanish and 0.3 per cent in other languages. It can be observed that the annual output is rather modest when compared with the output of certain neighbouring Arab countries. In terms of population, the annual output is 32.1 books per million people (see Table 4).

It will be seen from Table 4 that output during the early years was below the average for the entire period, but that it has risen during the past six years. The annual output of translations has also started to rise: the figure for 1978 is the same as for 1967, whereas output was more or less uniformly low during the intervening years.

OUTPUT BY SUBJECTS

From Table 5, it is clear that literature, the social sciences, history and geography together account for some three-quarters of total output. This almost exactly corresponds to the general position in the Arab world, and indicates the need to make up the deficiency in scientific, technical and philosophical subjects.

The subjects covered by the heading 'literature' include general studies, poetry, drama, fiction, essays, rhythmic prose, letters, books of anecdotes, humorous books and other categories. Poetry and fiction occupy an

TABLE 5.          Output of works by subject

| Subject | Number of books | Percentage of total |
| --- | --- | --- |
| Literature | 332 | 32.5 |
| Social sciences | 211 | 22.1 |
| History and geography | 212 | 22.1 |
| Religion | 79 | 8.7 |
| Technological sciences | 35 | 3.4 |
| General knowledge | 23 | 2.5 |
| Theoretical sciences | 15 | 1.6 |
| Arts and entertainment | 12 | 1.3 |
| Philosophy | 12 | 1.1 |
| Languages | 12 | 1.1 |
| Other subjects | 37 | 3.6 |

important place, whereas in the field of drama only fifteen plays have been published. The heading 'social sciences' covers civics, politics, economics, law, public administration, social services, education, business, popular literature and various other subjects. There was a conspicuous shortage of books about administration, education and business, especially the last-named, about which only five books were published. The heading 'history and geography' includes books on geography, travel, tourism, archaeology, biography and history. This suggests a shortage of books on the subjects of archaeology, tourism and geography. Jordan is a tourist country with many archaeological remains; there is therefore a need for books in these fields.

There are great shortages in the fields of religion, technological science, general knowledge, theoretical sciences, arts and entertainment, philosophy and languages. On the subject of agriculture, for example, only thirteen books have been published in Jordan in the past twelve years, even though Jordan is an agricultural country. General knowledge, theoretical sciences, and the other subjects mentioned are in much the same situation as the technological sciences.

## PUBLISHING AND PRINTING

At present, about 70 per cent of the general literary output is published in Jordan, and 30 per cent published abroad. Publishing in Jordan can be analysed as follows: public institutions, 35.5 per cent; the Department of Culture and Arts, 5.7 per cent; the Amman bookshop, 4.1 per cent; Philadelphia House, 3.5 per cent; the al-Aqsa bookshop, 2.7 per cent; the al-Muhtasab bookshop, 1.5 per cent; the Jordan Distribution Agency, 0.8 per cent; other sources, 6.1 per cent; and writers, 40 per cent.

This means that there are no publishing houses in the true sense, in Jordan. Philadelphia House tried to fill the role of a specialist publisher during the period 1974–76, but the venture was not a success. The other commercial bookshops are primarily trading organizations, not concerned with publishing. The Department of Culture and Arts, which is part of the Ministry of Culture and Youth, has assumed important responsibilities in connection with the publication of cultural and artistic magazines, and it is hoped that it will eventually play an even wider role in publishing literary works and distributing them in Jordan and abroad.

The above breakdown shows that the writers themselves, with 40 per cent of the total output, constitute the principal category of publishers in Jordan. The fact that so much of the load falls on writers will certainly continue to be a major obstacle to publishing. Clearly, there are many writers who want to publish their work, but hesitate before embarking on such a venture.

During the period under discussion, 294 books, representing about 30 per cent of total output, were published outside Jordan, in Lebanon, Egypt, the Syrian Arab Republic, Iraq, Iran, Saudi Arabia, Tunis, Qatar,

Libyan Arab Jamahiriya, Italy, the United Kingdom, the United States and other countries. In all probability, the reason for publishing some works outside Jordan is the existence of well-known publishing houses, as well as the high quality of production, marketing and distribution. Material published in Jordan is printed in Jordan, whereas material published abroad is printed abroad. The following presses have printed the majority of books in Jordan: The Co-operative Association of Printing Workers; the Jordanian Press; the Model Press; the Jordanian Press Organization; the Armed Forces Press; the Royal Society Press; and the Dar al-Sha'ab (House of the People) Press.

### DRAMA

The general public's reaction to the cultural decline, which started in the fifth century and continued until the beginning of the twentieth century, was to search for a dream related to a redeeming hero. This dream took many artistic forms. These forms included songs addressed to the prophet Muhammad, praising him, imploring his help and begging him to bring deliverance. They also included dramas dealing with the lone redeeming hero. The artistic form in which these dramas were cast was *al-Sira* (biography). The practitioners of this popular genre did not concern themselves with the famous heroes of history. Instead, they generally dealt with heroes who are mentioned in Arab Islamic history, but whose lives are not described in precise detail in this history, and whose existence cannot be firmly proved. Narratives of their lives were closer to heroic fiction than to history; indeed, it is doubtful whether any of these heroes really existed. The historical obscurity of their lives was an incentive to the popular narrator to infuse his own spirit and ideas, together with those of his community. The narrator used heroes to present an image of heroism and to depict heroic events. The lack of intellectual balance was a distinctive characteristic, which gave the narrator the chance to move into regions that literature had never previously dealt with. Justice and right were the basis of the intellectual structure of these works. Retribution, love, grace and redemption were terms scattered about the work, and around which the events of the drama revolved. This biographical form also had the advantage of offering an image of civilization to the groups of listeners who gathered in the coffee houses. These coffee houses in Irbid and Zarqa, for example, used to employ a professional popular story-teller. In al-Salt, Karak and other towns, in the period of Ottoman rule, before the great Arab revolt, people would also gather together at parties in private houses during the long rainy nights and listen to performances of this kind. For these people, *al-Sira* brought together all the concepts of civilization which remained from the earlier period of prosperity and brilliance. The important thing about this form was that it gave pleasure to the public; that is why it continued to exist even after the catastrophe of 1948. Perhaps the most significant achievement of *al-Sira* was to develop the art of acting, and so to prepare the way for the art of the theatre. The popular narrator took on the role of an actor, imitating the voices and movements of the different characters in the story. As the narrator's acting ability increased, so did the number of his admirers, and this process, in conjunction with a number of other cultural factors, led eventually to the emergence of the theatre proper. Drama was thus a natural development in Arab, and especially in Jordanian, society. *Al-Sira* first appeared as a substitute for fighting, and then in its turn gave rise to the art of acting. It is certainly true that contact with Western European civilization helped to speed up the development of drama. The modern period provided a propitious climate for the introduction of the European theatre to the Arab world, but this was in a sense only the enlargement of an endogenous process which had been taking place from about 1840 onwards, thanks to such writers as al-Nazzash, Sanna and al-Qabbani, who developed the art of *al-Sira* and raised it to new levels. Their influence spread from Egypt, Syria and Lebanon to most parts of the Arab world, including Palestine and Jordan. Nevertheless, the drama remained essentially popular in character being for the most part based on *al-Sira* as regards not only subject but narrative method. At the same time, however, plays translated from English or French were performed very differently from the Arab method. This left the theatre in a state of some confusion. Then academics turned their attention to this field, and wrote or adapted plays into which they introduced subject-matter not previously encountered in the Jordanian and Palestinian theatre. These writers included Shaikh Fuad al-Khatib (*The Conquest of Andalusia*), Husain Siraj (*The Passion of Wallada*) and Professor Husni Fariz (*The Flood*). Even before this, there had been considerable theatrical activity in Madaba, where the Association of Arab Catholic Youth was formed through the efforts of an Arab priest from Bethlehem called Antoine al-Hihi. The purposes of this association included acting. The group set up tents in the courtyard of the monastery, and presented three plays a year. The first play presented by this association was *The Landowner and the Devil*. This was followed by a local comedy and various other productions. Father Zakaria al-Shumli was responsible for eight productions during the period 1922–25, *The Merchant of Venice, Julius Caesar* and, in the field of indigenous drama, *Samuel—The Loyalty of the Arabs*. Entry to these plays was free, and they were well received by the people of Madaba. In al-Salt, Bishop Antoine Frighani, who was proficient in Arabic as an educated native speaker of the language, started a theatre in the building under the church. In 1928, he presented four plays, including *Saladin the Ayyubite*, which was performed on the day of the Festival of the Arab Awakening. The school at Ajlun, during this period, did work similar to that in Madaba and al-Salt; moreover, Ajlun was also fortunate in possessing the Okaz Club, whose activities covered a wide variety of fields including acting. According to Professor R. bin Zaid al-Uzaizi, this club, which had its own insignia and colours, enjoyed an outstanding reputation and its productions were highly successful. Attendance at them was free, and the open-air performances given in Ajlun and Madaba before the state established theatres in those cities, attracted large audiences.

The fact is that there was no theatre in Jordan when the state was established in 1921 by the Emir Abdullah bin Hussein, himself a writer and a poet. Dramatic activity was restricted to individual efforts. The Emir instructed his education officials to encourage artistic activities, especially historical drama, with the result that after some years the secondary schools in particular began to play an effective role in this field. Girls' schools, with their emphasis on social work, were especially active. Mrs Salwa Nasser Bshuti, who graduated from the Teachers' Institute in Jerusalem in 1928, says that the tribe of Beni Hassan were suffering from drought in 1930, so the teaching council of the Girls' School in Amman decided to put on a play and to allocate the profits to the poor people of the tribe. The play, produced under the patronage of the Emir Misbah, was *The Story of Samuel*. It was very well received by the ladies of Amman. Mrs Bshuti remembers that the costumes for the play were brought from a theatrical costumier in Jerusalem. Members of the teaching staff took the male parts, together with some of the young ladies of the community. Another play, *Saladin the Ayyubite* was put on for the benefit of the same tribe, and very soon after that a third play was presented, this time on the stage of the Petra cinema and before an exclusively female audience. This does not mean, however, that girls' schools were the only schools to put on plays. The secondary school at al-Salt had historical-drama seasons during which the plays performed included *Haroun al-Rashid, Ali Bek al-Kebir*, and *Antony and Cleopatra*. As secondary education spread throughout the kingdom, the secondary schools of Irbid, Karak and other cities also put on successful plays; and in addition to this, the cultural associations which developed in Amman, Irbid and al-Salt presented a number of dramatic works from time to time in their modest theatres. These were the places which brought educated people together from the early 1950s. It can therefore be said that the school theatre played an important part in the history of the Jordanian theatre, especially during this period, when close co-operation developed between the private sector (represented by the work of individuals and literary clubs) and the public sector (represented by the schools, which were spreading throughout the country).

This co-operation resulted in a number of plays which were mainly presented on school stages. The cultural and literary clubs and charitable associations based in Amman, Irbid, Zarqa, al-Salt, Madaba and Ajlun did commendable work, presenting plays by Jordanian, Arab and international writers, and attracting the most cultivated elements of Jordanian society to these performances.

The theatre continued to develop along these lines until the establishment of the University of Jordan in 1962, when the University of Jordan

Theatre Company came into being. This company began work immediately after the creation of the university, presenting shows which included scenes from plays. During the first three years of its existence, the university developed rapidly, acquiring a faculty of Science and a faculty of Economics and Business in addition to the original faculty of Letters. All this had a great effect in stimulating extracurricular activities, including drama, where a start was made with a play presented by the faculty of Economics and Business in 1966. This student production was enthusiastically received, and the university then called in Hani Snauber, the teacher of dramatic production, who found that the university's students had excellent creative potential and were very adaptable material. Under his guidance, further student productions were mounted in 1967 and 1968. In discussing these productions, Professor Yaghi draws a parallel with the work of the mid-nineteenth-century pioneers of the Arab theatre, who on occasion borrowed material from other sources but made it their own by the skill with which they translated it and adapted it to suit their purposes.

In 1968, a locally written play was presented in the university theatre by Jamal Abu Hamdan. The play was by a Jordanian writer, the production was Jordanian, and the actors were students of the university. So the Jordanian theatre acquired a new dimension. The university theatre attracted artistic talents that had been looking for an organization to promote them. The next outstanding event was a production of Bernard Shaw's *Arms and the Man* (in translation) by the Department of English theatre group. A large number of actors progressed to the front rank from the start of 1969 onwards. In that year, the Faculty of Sciences entered the field, putting on Albert Camus's play *Les Justes*. Further productions followed, and in the middle of May 1971 a number of other plays were produced by the various university faculties. The great year for drama in the university, however, was 1972, when a large number of plays were presented, with each faculty endeavouring to outdo the other. This produced a positive interaction between the educated public and the actors. Perhaps the most distinctive feature of the theatre at this time was that it broke away from the tradition that had prevented women from appearing on stage alongside men. The university theatre undoubtedly rendered an important service to drama in Jordan, not least as a nursery of artistic talent which continues to influence the progress of the Jordanian theatre. The theatre continues to develop rapidly, especially since the cross-fertilization of Jordanian ideas with those introduced by foreign groups such as the American Information Centre Drama Group, who appeared in a production of *Cat on a Hot Tin Roof* in October 1968.

The Jordanian Theatre Company acquired its name and official status in 1964 following a performance of Robert Thomas's play *The Trap* at which the Minister for Culture and Information happened to be present. According to Hani Snauber, the minister was so impressed that he at once invited the players to call on him at the ministry and there formed them into a state-sponsored theatre company, supported materially and in other ways by the Ministry of Culture and Information and attached to the Department of Culture and Arts.

The company's activities fall into three categories: traditional theatre: (performances of international plays in translation), childrens' theatre, and an annual dramatic and operatic festival.

*Traditional theatre*. Productions in this category were mainly the work of Hani Snauber, whose aim has been to strike a balance between the theatre as entertainment and as a vehicle for dealing with issues. His influence can be seen in the work of younger producers such as Ahmad Quadari, Ahmad Shaqm and Hatim al-Said (although the last-named is more inclined towards the avant-garde, committed theatre).

*Children's theatre*. Here the guiding spirit has been the producer Margot Malatjilian. Her first production was a play called *Anbara and the Witch*, which was followed by *The Dancing Donkey* and *The Wood-cutter's Children*. This producer had mastered the art of working with child actors, and her balanced approach has ensured beneficial results. The success of the first three plays led to further productions, including *The Piper* and *Master and Servant*.

*Opera* was introduced to Jordan through the annual festivals established first at Ramallah and later at Ariha. The programmes for these events were composed by Abd al-Rahim Amr, whose opera *Khalida* was staged in 1971 on the occasion of the fiftieth anniversary of the establishment of the kingdom. The producer was Hani Snauber, and the opera was presented on the stage of the Palace of Culture. Further productions by the Jordanian Theatre Company have included such works as *Fathers and Sons*. Nor was opera limited to productions by the Jordanian Theatre Company. Folk operas were staged in Jerusalem by the House of the Arab Child and brought to Ramallah and al-Bira by a touring company.

The opera *Khalida* was Hani Snauber's first experiment with a work involving singing dancing and the spoken word. It was also a new departure for the Department of Culture and Arts, which encouraged the Popular Arts Group to contribute tableaux depicting scenes of everyday life in Jordan. In addition to the above-mentioned companies, various private groups established in the 1960s and 1970s, such as the Theatre Group, the Golden Theatre Group, the Popular Theatre Group, the Starlight Group, the Ammun 74 Theatre Group and the Amman Training Centre Group, also put on performances, but without attaining such a high standard. Perhaps the most prominent of these groups was the Ammun 74 Theatre Group, which played an active role in the private-sector theatre and made a memorable appearance on the stage of the Palace of Culture. The Amman Training Centre used to hold an open day, displaying the various facets of its activities, including plays presented by the students. Among the impressive productions mounted in this way, was one of Shakespeare's

73

*Merchant of Venice.* The Starlight Group also did excellent work. In general, however, these groups were not able to keep abreast of developments in the serious theatre or to tackle plays dealing with national and social problems. The university theatre, too, began to encounter difficulties, while the private-sector theatre fell into a state of decline and moved further and further away from the current social and human preoccupations of society.

This was the state of affairs confronting the newly established Ministry of Culture and Youth, which realized that it must take the initiative as regards the theatre, and play its part in the long-term education of the general public. It accordingly instructed the Department of Culture and Arts to open an experimental theatre school, in the summer of 1977, to train actors who could provide a basis for the development of a contemporary national theatre, with a distinctive character and with roots in the local environment.

The ministry also participated in the creation of a League of Jordanian Theatre Workers on 31 December 1977, thereby establishing a solid basis for the theatrical profession. The minister had already issued an order dissolving all the committees attached to the drama section of the Department of Culture and Arts, the aim being to reorganize the section in a manner appropriate to the demands of cultural development in Jordan, and thereby contribute to the advancement of the theatre. One result of this, was the introduction of a regular system of contracts of employment instead of monthly salaries, as well as the appointment of a number of producers as university teachers specializing in drama. The Minister of Culture and Youth set up a drama committee composed of leading drama teachers, of which he was chairman and attended by the Director-General of the Department of Culture and Arts. This committee prepared a long-term plan for promoting high-quality drama; for fostering awareness of the theatre; for approving scripts and checking proofs; for giving advice to producers and encouraging them to participate in conferences, study groups and seminars so as to raise their level of technical competence; for taking the theatre from the capital to the provinces in co-operation with the Youth Welfare Organization, etc.

As a result of these endeavours, the Department of Culture and Arts was able, for the first time in the history of the country, to organize a complete theatrical season, beginning in October 1977 and going on to the end of June 1978. Nine plays (two by Jordanians, four by other Arab dramatists and three by non-Arabs) were presented in the department's own theatre, most of them being subsequently taken on tour under the auspices of the department acting in co-operation with the youth centres operated by the Youth Welfare Organization.

The season culminated in the holding of the first Jordanian Seminar on the Theatre, on the initiative of the Minister for Culture and Youth. This seminar, which was held in the Palace of Culture in the al-Hussein

Youth Complex in Amman from 19 to 23 August 1978, and was the first of its kind in the history of the theatre in Jordan, aroused keen interest in educated circles and received extensive press, radio and television coverage. In his opening remarks, the minister re-stated his ministry's cultural policy in detail, and drew attention to the role of the cultural worker and the importance of co-operation between the various organizations.

The seminar produced a number of very important recommendations concerning: the need to create a high-quality theatre which would deal with human problems and would address the widest possible public; the importance of encouraging Jordanian playwrights, and of care in the selection of plays by them and by foreign playwrights, both Arab and non-Arab; the Royal Theatre, which, with its up-to-date facilities and techniques would be the spearhead of a national drama movement involving other theatres in the various cultural centres to be established throughout the country. At the end of the seminar, the Minister for Culture and Youth observed that the level of discussion throughout the proceedings had been high and distinguished by a strong sense of responsibility.

The seminar was certainly an effective move towards developing a contemporary Jordanian theatre with the mission of reaching a wide segment of the public. It enabled the Ministry of Culture and Youth to clarify its objectives and to set in motion a process of constructive inter-action aimed at developing the theatre and moulding its character, on the basis that the theatre is a group activity requiring public involvement in order to attain its full maturity.

The Jordanian theatre is now on the road to important achievements, following the creation of the Ministry of Culture and Youth. According to recent statistics published in the magazine *Arts*, there are some twenty playwrights active in Jordan, and roughly the same number of producers. During the past ten to twelve years, eighty-two plays have been produced, including forty-five by Jordanian writers. All this shows that the theatre has acquired a new dimension, which is bound to affect its further development and assure it a wide audience both at home and abroad.

## Folklore

The Jordanian character shows itself in a range of distinctive and varied folklore. The country is clearly a region with unusual characteristics. This does not mean that Jordan does not share these characteristics with its Arab neighbours; but it is the sum total of these features which gives Jordan its distinctive character.

Jordan is linked to many regions without being completely in any of them. It is at the crossroads between Asia and Africa. It has mountains, plains, desert and sea. It is in the desert but not of the desert; rather, it is an oasis supplying the desert. This exceptional diversity has certainly been reflected in Jordan's popular traditions; there are Bedouin, rural and city traditions. Each of these milieux has its beliefs, values, social traditions, music, dance, literature, industries and crafts, folk medicine, etc.

During the past twenty-five years, a number of bodies in Jordan have been engaged in safeguarding and fostering this heritage. The Department of Tourism, the Department of Antiquities, the Ministry of Education and Instruction, the Ministry of Culture and Information and subsequently the Ministry of Culture and Youth were all concerned with this work. Article 3(b) of Statute No. 1 of 1977, concerning the Ministry of Culture and Youth, specifies the need to revive and disseminate the Arab heritage in the sciences, literature and the arts, including the popular arts. Law No. 10 of 1968 concerning the Ministry of Tourism stated the need for supervision of traditional industries. Article 4 of Law No. 16 of 1964 on Education mentions the need to develop aspects of Jordanian and Arab popular art. Article 5 of the same law, calls for the encouragement of all forms of popular art and the fine arts, both within and outside the educational system. This is in addition to the provisions of the regulations concerning clubs and museums specializing in the popular heritage. As for the University of Jordan, Article 5(e) of Law No. 52 of 1972 refers to the need to develop the national heritage. During the past twenty-five years, and even earlier, works on folklore have been produced in Jordan by both the private and public sectors. The work of the private sector began in 1923 with the publication of a number of works on folklore including the book, *Things I Have Seen and Heard*, by Khair al-Din al-Zarkali. This writer published another book in 1925 entitled *Two Years in Amman*. These two books were not specialist works, but they contained some general reflections on folklore. In 1929, the Archimandrite Paulos Sam'an published a book entitled *Five Years East of the Jordan*, dealing with some of the customs and traditions followed in the East-bank region. He also described the various tribes of the region and gave details of Bedouin customs, traditions, morals and sayings. The only relevant work published in the 1930s was Frederick J. Beck's *History of the Region East of the Jordan and of its Tribes*, in a translation by Baha' al-Din Tuqan. The second section of the book deals with the Bedouin tribes. No works on folklore were published during the 1940s, because of the Second World War and the Arab-Israeli war. However, Jordanians were able to listen to *Sira* (bibliographical narrative) performances and to readings of the poems of Mustapha Wahbi al-Tell, which, despite the classical nature of their language, were full of popular expressions and terms, colloquial sayings and local jokes, so that they were close to the mentality of the general public. In the 1950s, there was the study by Rukus bin Zaid al-Azizi called *The Prey of Abu Madi* (1956), which gave full weight to the value and importance of the Bedouin heritage. During the same decade, Dr Butrus Baz published a collection of popular sayings, and Tawfiq abu al-Su'ud produced a story entitled *King Saif bin dhi Yazn*. In the 1960s, a number of books on folklore were published, including *Madaba and its Environs* and *A Collection of Popular Stories* by Professor Faiz Ali al-Ghul, as well as *Songs from Jordan, Popular Songs from the East Bank, Popular Songs from the West Bank* and *Jordanian Popular Sayings*. It can indeed be said that there was now a full range of books on folklore, in that there were more than seventy-five covering most aspects.

On the official side, the Department of Culture and Arts, even though it was established rather late, was able to do a great deal for Jordanian popular traditions, including the drafting of a preliminary plan for their collection. The department began to implement this plan with effect from the middle of 1968, and it continued in operation until the middle of 1970. An example of this work was the collection of 115 hours of recordings of popular songs from all parts of the kingdom. The department did not resume its activities in this field until 1974, when it began to record the work of a number of popular poets. This phase continued until the middle of 1975, when the department turned its attention to recording collections of material about the life of the people in various regions of the kingdom, and published these collections in the magazine *Popular Arts*, which appeared in 1974. In the middle of 1977, the department began to send a number of missions to various areas to collect examples of folklore. It also implemented a plan for creating an archive of traditions for the purpose of recording aspects of Jordanian popular life, as a source of reference for specialists and students. The sayings of a number of elderly men in many different areas were recorded in this way. The department appointed correspondents on folklore in most areas of the kingdom, and a start was made on the recording of material according to a predetermined schedule; the amount of material recorded under this arrangement during a single year exceeded 1,400 hours.

The magazine *Ideas* started publication in 1966, and soon began to carry studies and articles dealing with popular traditions. At the same time, the department produced a number of publications and booklets, as well as specialized works dealing with specific aspects of Jordanian traditions. It formed artistic groups which travelled all over the country, giving performances of popular dances. These groups have also worked outside Jordan, and have performed in most Arab theatres and elsewhere. We must mention here the role of the Radio Service, which has been and continues to be a pioneer in the fostering of the nation's literary and other traditions. Its involvement in this sphere first became evident during the directorship of Hiza' al-Majali and Wasfi al-Tell. The popular material collected and arranged by Professor Rashid Zaid al-Kilani featured prominently in radio programmes. The Radio Service still plays a major role, broadcasting programmes on folklore which provide a picture of Jordanian popular life and art in all their varied aspects.

The Jordanian Television Service has also done notable work in this field, broadcasting numerous highly successful programmes, based on field research, regarding the social, cultural and other aspects of popular tradition. This has called for an informed awareness of the enormous influence of writing, and the other arts on the life of the individual Jordanian and of Jordanian society, together with a keen perception of performance techniques, involving attention to words, gestures, movement and rhythm, together with scrupulous fidelity to the original. This is where the work of the Jordanian Television Service has been most conspicuous. It has filmed some of its material on the spot, and has presented programmes dealing with specific aspects of popular life, as well as serializations of popular stories. It has also turned its attention to the visual arts and has broadcast programmes about costumes, crafts, etc.

Programmes featuring the work of a number of Jordanian researchers including Rukus bin Zaid al-Azizi, Nimr Sarhan and Ahmad Awidi al-Abadi, have been shown on television with such success that copies of them have been purchased for retransmission by the television services of neighbouring Arab countries.

Turning to clubs, we find that a number of these were formed from the 1960s onwards, specializing in the conservation of examples of folklore. It appears that one reason for this was the growth of national sentiment, which impelled the authorities to take the initiative in creating clubs and centres to organize work for promoting, conserving and presenting the artistic heritage.

The first club established for this purpose was the Club for the Revival of the Jordanian Popular Heritage, which held its first exhibition in the summer of 1971, showing examples of folk costumes from both banks of the Jordan. It also collected examples of jewellery, traditional implements, etc.

In 1972, the Roman amphitheatre in Amman was chosen, on account of its historical importance and its popularity with tourists, as the site of the Museum of Traditional Costumes and Jewellery. This museum has the objective of preserving our popular heritage from destruction, and of making the people of Jordan aware that their country and their community have a long and splendid history; it also aims at developing appreciation of the beauty and importance of the heritage.

The museum (whose objectives and financial and administrative organization are regulated by statute) contains examples of folk costumes from different parts of the kingdom, with jewellery, furniture, handicraft products, carpets, embroidery and a wide variety of copper utensils. Exhibitions of folk costumes have been organized on several occasions.

The Museum of Popular Life, administered by the Department of Antiquities, has two sections. The first section concentrates on collecting and displaying to the public examples of the popular heritage in the form of jewellery and costumes. The second section represents Jordanian popular life in all its aspects. This section depicts the life of the desert and of the countryside, both in Jordan and in the occupied territory. Its statutes were promulgated in 1974.

The Centre for Handicrafts was established a few years ago in order to encourage Jordanian crafts and craftsmen. Its principal aims include: reproducing traditional popular artefacts; encouraging craftsmen and marketing their products; developing crafts industries along contemporary lines; participating effectively in the Jordanian crafts academy, and representing Jordan in the World Crafts Council so as to explain the characteristics of Jordanian traditional handicrafts.

The Department of Culture and Arts has a Popular Museum, for which its field researchers started to collect suitable objects in 1968. The Five-year Plan gave high priority to reviving the Jordanian popular heritage, and recommended the establishment of a Jordanian centre for popular arts. This centre will include a section for printed material and another section for recordings and films, in addition to an archive section and a specialist folklore library.

Concern for popular traditions in Jordan does not stop there. A valuable contribution is also made by various official and non-official agencies, by a number of specialists in popular traditions who are engaged in defining the styles and characteristics of popular art, and by the different industries responsible for giving expression to popular culture, in its material aspects. All these people and organizations intend to participate in implementing a plan to survey the whole of Jordan, to record its traditions and to make the results available to researchers for further study.

With this aim in view, the Ministry of Culture and Youth (created to sponsor popular culture and arts) has decided to carry out the necessary surveying, recording, preparation, indexing and classification, as well as sponsoring specialists and publishing their output. The ministry has legislation aimed at promoting culture in all its forms. It has instituted a system of state awards in recognition of achievement, to encourage projects and publishing. This recently created ministry hopes to set up a folklore complex—possibly including actual residential and working accommodation for artisans—together with a museum of popular life, covering popular styles of building, Bedouin and peasant domestic utensils, furniture and costumes, and illustrations of social, religious and commercial life.

The museum would be able to play a larger role if an institute for teaching folklore were attached to it, together with a systematic archive of folklore material. The institute could publish museum catalogues and directories of craftsmen and, it could also set up a library containing printed material, written records, voice recordings, photographs, films, music, and specialist reports and other documents connected with popular traditions. In all probability, this may come about in the context of an overall plan for the collection, recording, classification and conservation of popular traditions.

In addition to publishing books and creating official and non-official clubs and museums, the official organizations concerned with the preservation of popular traditions also produced specialist magazines. At the beginning of 1974, the Department of Culture and Arts in Amman brought out a special magazine devoted to the Jordanian popular heritage. The producers of this magazine have worked to free the heritage from undesirable accretions and to bring to light unknown aspects of it, especially in the oral and visual spheres.

A committee for research on society and the Palestinian popular heritage, the al-Bira Community Revival Association, founded in 1965 in the West bank, has published a magazine on social affairs and the popular heritage. This magazine first appeared in April 1974. It is important for three reasons. First, it appears in the occupied territory, where deliberate attempts by Israel are being made to obliterate the traces of our history, both on the official and on the popular level, as well as our holy places and religious beliefs and anything remotely connected with our traditions and social and economic customs. Secondly, the magazine's special aim, in conformity with the goals and aspirations of the community and in accordance with a correct understanding of the role of the subjective factor is to distil and understand the real essence of the popular Palestinian heritage by all available means, irrespective of language. Thirdly, the committee aims to collect everything it can in the way of tools and utensils used by our ancestors, such as domestic and agricultural implements, equipment used in games, sports and folk medicine, as well as weapons, etc.

Jordanian women have been no less active than Jordanian men in the field of popular traditions. Conspicuous examples are Mrs Wasfi al-Tell, President of the Club for the Revival of the Jordanian Popular Heritage, and of the Council of Administration of the Museum of Traditional Costumes and Jewellery; Mrs Hind Manku, President of the Centre for Handicrafts; Mrs Jansit Shami, the eminent sculptress who was among the founder members of the Royal Jordanian Fine Arts Association and of the Jordanian Folklore Association; Mrs Widad Qi'war, the authority on traditional costumes and jewellery; and Miss Hadiya Ibadha, a former secretary of the Museum of the Department of Antiquities and a founder member of the Club for the Revival of the Jordanian Heritage.

The Department of Antiquities helped with the financing, organization and cataloguing of the Museum of Popular Life, which opened in 1975, and has also taken an active interest in the Museum of Traditional Life which it is proposed to establish in Madaba.

The establishment of local museums in Irbid, al-Salt, Madaba and other cities will make it possible to display the heritage of each area independently. It will then be possible to study the points of similarity and dissimilarity between the northern, central and southern parts of the country. Miss Hadiya Ibadha hopes in due course to classify the contents of the various museums and to make them into folklore research centres for the study of costumes, implements, music and musical instruments, etc.

Behind the official and individual concern for folklore, there is probably a profound feeling that the modern age, with its rapid developments, has started to threaten our nation's traditional way of life in its various aspects, and that steps must be taken to preserve the element of continuity, and the values enshrined in the popular heritage.

## The Visual Arts

There was little activity in this field before the establishment of modern Jordan. Since then, the visual-arts movement has gone through a number of stages, and there is now a generation of committed Jordanian artists who combine awareness of their heritage with the ability to see their work in the context of the problems, desires, dreams and aspirations of the individual, the community, the Arab nation and the world as a whole.

The beginning of this movement, which attained maturity in the 1950s, dates back to the work of two artists, Omar al-Unsi and Diya' al-Din Suleiman, who flourished during the 1930s (the only artists to work in Jordan before that time had been foreigners—e.g. David Roberts—who toured the country drawing and painting the places visited by tourists). Suleiman's exhibition at the Philadelphia Hotel in 1938 was probably the first of its kind in Jordan. This artist was a prolific painter, and his contemporary, Omar al-Unsi, was famous for his water-colours.

At the start of the 1950s, a number of painters appeared, including Anton Basil, Sami Ni'meh and Ihsan Idilbi. In association with Valeria Sha'ban, these artists held a seminar on the visual arts at the Nahda Institute in Amman. A visual-arts section, including pictures by Fatima Muhib, Rebecca Bahu and Valeria Sha'ban, was attached to the industrial and agricultural exhibition held at the Islamic College in Amman, in 1952. An exhibition by a group of painters in Amman—probably the first of its kind—was held in the Arab Club under the patronage of its president, Sheikh Ibrahim Qattan. In 1954, exhibitions were held at the Cultural Co-operation Club and others at the al-Uruba school in Irbid in 1955. The work of this generation of artists was characterized by its close connection with the realist style. There is no doubt that the catastrophe of 1948 has an important influence on the trends followed by most artists during this period.

Perhaps the most prominent artist to appear at this time was George Alief, whose pupils included Rafiq Lahham, Mohanna Durra, Da'ad al-Tal and Nayla Deeb. Alief opened a school of music and painting at which many amateurs received instruction, among them Sharif Abdul-Hamid Sharaf and Dr Ihsan Daghistani.

It was not long before a new generation of artists who had studied abroad returned to Jordan bringing with them a fresh concept of contemporary art. This generation quickly made its presence felt in artistic life. Although the established artistic style continued to enjoy a high level of public response and acceptance, the newer trends also began to be accepted by the public so that the artistic movement in general and the visual arts in particular were impelled to go forward. The first League of Arts and Literature, with Saif Uddin Kilani and Ghalib Barakat among its members, was established in Amman in 1962, and held a number of exhibitions both there and in Jerusalem. The works of artists at this time were characterized by new techniques. Group exhibitions were held by academics such as Ali al-Ghul and Mohanna Durra, Afaf Arafat, Rafiq Lahham, Ahmad Ni'wash and others.

In the 1970s, scholarship students who had been sent by the Ministry of Education to study art in Egypt, Iraq and Italy returned to Jordan. The Royal Fine Arts Society was established and held one-man shows and group exhibitions, including one that brought together the work of twelve Jordanian artists.

The Department of Culture and Arts had already been set up. Its statutes stressed the importance of supporting artists, of buying some of their work and of encouraging them by holding individual and group exhibitions. The department's Institute of Fine Arts set up training courses, seminars and exhibitions. Distinctive styles began to appear. Rabah Sughayar and others discussed artistic problems in the press and other media. Discussions and dialogues on art became more frequent, helping to develop the movement, and acquainting the public with the artists and their work. The arts can be said to have attained their full maturity in Jordan in the mid-1970s. At the end of 1976, the Ministry of Culture and Youth was established, and took responsibility for encouraging artistic talent and supporting creative tendencies in the arts. Indeed, the first meeting between the Minister for Culture and Youth and Jordanian artists took place very soon after the creation of the ministry. The artists began to make plans for setting up their own league, and a fine-arts section was established in the Department of Culture and Arts. In 1977, a number of art exhibitions were held in Jordan and abroad, including one of works by Ahmad Ni'wash at Unesco headquarters in Paris.

Other exhibition subjects included Spanish Islamic drawings, works by Jordanian artists trained in Italy, paintings of King Hussein spanning a period of twenty-five years, paintings by Japanese children, Syrian art and coloured photographs of Jordan. In the same year, the first Jordanian Fine Arts Exhibition was held. This brought together works by thirty-seven Jordanian artists representing the whole spectrum of contemporary artistic trends.

In 1978, the ministry organised seventeen exhibitions. The most important of these was certainly the second Fine Arts Exhibition, in which fifty-two artists exhibited, showing 160 pictures. There were also important and varied exhibitions of architecture, and photography.

The applied arts too—pottery, glasswork, mosaics, needlework, weaving, etc.—have recently attracted considerable attention. Artists have experimented with different combinations of local materials, and the resulting works of arts have shown the unmistakable influence of the

Jordanian environment and popular traditions, as well as a keen sense of the aesthetic importance of the co-ordination of line and colour.

Painting is, of all the arts, perhaps the one which has been most favoured with attention. Most Jordanian painters have contributed fresh ideas to the art of painting, together with new expertise resulting from the techniques they have studied and which accord with the concept of the linking of form to content. A number of Jordanian painters have held exhibitions in Jordan and abroad. Each artist has given evidence of his own particular style. Many of them have dealt with pressing human problems, while several have concentrated more particularly on the Israeli occupation and the tragedy of the refugees.

While impressionism, cubism and other schools have had their individual followings, some painters have tried to combine the various schools, and to create new tendencies in art, with a balance between appearance, form and content, and a basic emphasis on compositional values.

Anyone who has looked at the work of these pioneer artists will be aware of the effort that has gone into it. The younger generation of artists has also shown great promise. Perhaps the common denominator between both groups is the fact that they depict the Jordanian and Arab environments in all their aspects. Attempts continue to be made to go back to the original roots of Arab Islamic art, and an academic spirit appears at times to preponderate in many works, but even here the influence of the Iraqi, Egyptian and Italian schools is still manifest.

It is worth noting that various foreign centres in Jordan, including the British, American, French and Soviet cultural centres, and the Goethe Institute, have performed a valuable service for the arts by arranging exhibitions, as have Jordanian bodies such as the Palace of Culture in the al-Hussein Youth Complex, the Library of the University of Jordan, the Princess Hayya Cultural Centre, etc. All these centres have held one-man and group exhibitions of the works of Jordanian and foreign artists. When the Ministry of Culture and Youth moved to a permanent building, a hall was set aside in the ministry for exhibitions. This demonstrated the ministry's awareness and appreciation of the role played by art in contemporary Jordanian life.

A League of Artists was formed, with the material and moral support of the Ministry of Culture and Youth, as from the start of 1977. Statute No. 19 of 1977 concerning state prizes in recognition of achievement in literature and the arts (issued in accordance with Article 114 of the Constitution) specifies that the state certificate in recognition of achievement and/or the cash prize shall be granted in many fields, including the visual arts, and two visual artists did in fact win, respectively, the entire prize for 1977 and half the prize for 1978. The Ministry of Culture and Youth seeks to promote the arts and to encourage their development in the interests of a better life and an advanced, harmonious society, both in Jordan and in the world as a whole.

83

## Music

Jordan occupies a distinctive position in the Arab world. From the earliest times, it has been a meeting point for trading caravans and other travellers. Civilizations resembling those of neighbouring countries have been established in Jordan, including the Ammonite and Nabataean civilizations, and other cultures, which took an interest in music and the fine arts.

After the Islamic conquests, a new musical culture was established in Jordan under the patronage of the Ummayads, the Abbasids and the other Islamic caliphs. When, in the twentieth century, the modern Jordanian state was created, the authorities did everything possible to promote and encourage music, for which a new day can be said to have dawned. The foundations were laid for a full-scale musical revival with the formation of the Jordanian Radio Group in Amman, the expansion of the Department of Military Music, the establishment of the Institute of Music, the formulation of musical development plans by the Ministry of Culture and Youth, and the decision by the Ministry of Education and Instruction to include music in the curriculum of the Amman Teacher-training College.

The Jordanian Radio Service has played an important part in taking the musical heritage from the limited environment of the village and the desert, and bringing it to the listening public. It has had the task of conserving and disseminating the heritage, as well as helping to encourage instrumental and vocal composition. The same can be said of the Jordanian Television Service.

The Institute of Music was established in 1966 as an independent section in the Department of Culture and Arts (Ministry of Culture and Youth). It started by teaching music to various groups of amateurs and has been taking students on a regular basis since 1973. Throughout its various departments (strings, woodwind, pianoforte, Arab instruments, theory of music) the institute uses a syllabus in which Arab and non-Arab music are combined.

The Jordanian theatre has also presented a number of operas, including *The Bride of Evil Omen* by Abd Allah al-Barghuti, produced at the Ramallah festival in 1964. Abd al-Rahim Amr and Jamil al-'As, with the members of the Jordanian Radio Group and the Jordanian Popular Arts Group, have also presented operas with national themes in connection with the Festival of Oranges at Ariha. Two other operas by Abd al-Rahim Amr, *Khalida* and *Fathers and Sons*, also enjoyed great success, as did *The Demon of Wealth*, presented by Sabra al-Sharif and Tawfiq al-Basha.

The Ministry of Education and Instruction has also done much to promote musical activities. It regards music as an important element in education, and the curriculum produced in 1965 for the compulsory and preparatory stage, provided for weekly instruction in the subject. In 1975, the Council for Education decided to begin training music teachers, and special courses were introduced at the Teacher-training Institute in

Amman. The private schools too regard music as a fundamental part of their syllabus and endeavour to encourage artistic talent.

The Jordanians have inherited their Arab ancestors' love of military music. An army band was started in 1940 and in 1945, its strength was increased to seventeen. In 1950, a number of musicians were specially recruited as bandsmen. In 1952, the band was modernized and re-equipped, and in 1955 it made a four-month tour of the United Kingdom and took part in the international brass-band festival there. It then went on to give prize-winning performances. A number of subsequent improvements to the band, included the addition of stringed instruments to the existing wind and percussion groups. It also began to tackle more advanced scores.

The Jordanian Army Band serves in many different places. It is present at the arrival and departure of important official guests and plays appropriate music on major national occasions. It has given public performances, and has helped private and state schools to develop their musical activities. It has given technical advice to a number of Arab countries, recorded various marches and similar items, and participated in the recording of traditional and other songs for radio and television.

Music in Jordan is by no means merely secular, but constitutes, in the form of sacred song, an important traditional element in many religious services and celebrations, both Muslim and Christian.

Folk music, too, continues to flourish in every part of the country. At weddings, for example, one encounters all sorts of traditional songs, as well as traditional dances and plays, and mothers still rock their children to sleep with the ever-fresh traditional lullabies.

# Bibliography

ANON. *Our Culture During 50 Years.* Amman, Department of Culture and Arts, 1972.

MINISTRY OF CULTURE AND INFORMATION. *Jordan During 50 Years.* Amman, Department of Printed Material and Publishing, 1972.

MINISTRY OF EDUCATION AND INSTRUCTION. *The Development of Education in Jordan.* Amman, Department of Printed Material and Publishing, 1977.

NATIONAL PLANNING COUNCIL. *Cultural Agreements.* Amman, National Planning Council, 1977.

——. *The 1976–80 Five-year Development Plan.* Amman, Royal Scientific Society Press, 1977.

YAHYA SHAGAWARA, D. *Information and National Development.* Amman, Royal Scientific Society, 1978.

The serial numbering of titles in this series, the presentation of which has been
modified, was discontinued with the volume *Cultural policy in Italy*